Sun Technical Reference Library

James Gosling
David S.H. Rosenthal
Michelle J. Arden

The NeWS Book

An Introduction to the
Network/extensible Window System

Springer-Verlag
New York Berlin Heidelberg
London Paris Tokyo Hong Kong

James Gosling
David S.H. Rosenthal
Michelle J. Arden
Sun Microsystems, Inc.
Mountain View, CA 94043, USA

Graphics Designer and Editor: David A. LaVallée

Sun Workstation, SunWindows, SunView, Sun-1, Sun-2, NeWS, NDE, X11/NeWs, Network File System, Open Fonts, F3, Typemaker, TypeScaler, and the Sun logo are registered trademarks of Sun Microsystems, Incorporated. PostScript is a registered trademark of Adobe Systems, Incorporated. X Window System is a registered trademark of Massachussetts Institute of Technology. UNIX and OPEN LOOK are registered Trademarks of AT&T.

Quickdraw, Macintosh, Switcher, Finder, and MacApp are trademarks of Apple Computer. Mathematica is a trademark of Wolfram Research; Inc. OS/2, Presentation Manager, MS/DOS, LAN Manager, and MSWindows are trademarks of Microsoft Corporation. Atari is a trademark of Atari Corporation. Amiga is a trademark of Commodore. Andrew is a trademark of Carnegie Mellon University. VAX, PDP-10, MicroVax, and VMS are trademarks of Digital Equipment Corporation. Smalltalk, Alto, Dorado, DLisp, Star, Viewers, Interlisp-D, Ethernet, Mesa, Cedar, Pilot, Tajo, and Docs are trademarks of Xerox Corporation. Interpress is a trademark of Imagen. PC/RT us a trademark of IBM. GEM is a trademark of Digital Research, Inc. EXPRES is a trademark of NSF. Multics is a trademark of Honeywell. Parallax 1280 and Viper are trademarks of Parallax Graphics, Inc. Silicon Graphics, IRIS 4D, 4sight, and the SGI logo are registered trademarks of Silicon Graphics, Inc. NeWS/2 is a trademark of Architech Corporation. Times-Roman, Courier, New Century Schoolbook, Snell Roundhand, and Helvetica are trademarks of Linotype. The NeWS Cookbook is a trademark of Pica Pty. Ltd. All other products listed in this book are trademarks of their companies.

Sun Microsystems, Inc., has reviewed the contents of this book prior to final publication. The book does not necessarily represent the views, opinions, or product strategies of the Company or its subsidaries. Sun is not responsible for its contents or its accuracy, and therefore makes no representations or warranties with respect to it. Sun believes, however, that it presents accurate and valuable information to the interested reader, as of the time of publication.

Sun trademarks and product names referred to herein are proprietary to Sun.

Library of Congress Cataloging-in-Publication Data
Gosling, James
    The NeWS book : an introduction to the Networked Extensible Window
System / James Gosling, David S.H. Rosenthal, Michelle J. Arden.
        p. cm.—(The Sun technical reference library)
    Bibliography: p.
    Includes index.
    ISBN 0-387-96915-2
    1. Windows (Computer programs) 2. NeWS (Computer program)
I. Rosenthal, David S.H. II. Arden, Michelle J. III. Title.
IV. Series.
QA76.76.W56A73   1989
005.4'3—dc20   89-11329

Camera-ready copy prepared by the authors.
Printed and bound by R.R. Donnelley & Sons, Harrisonburg, Virginia.
Printed in the United States of America.

9 8 7 6 5 4 3 2 1 Printed on acid free paper.

ISBN 0-387-96915-2 Springer-Verlag New York Berlin Heidelberg
ISBN 3-540-96915-2 Springer-Verlag Berlin Heidelberg New York

Preface

This book is an introduction to NeWS: the Networked, Extensible, Window System from Sun Microsystems. It is oriented towards people who have a basic knowledge of programming and window systems who would like to understand more about window systems in general and NeWS in particular. A significant portion of the book is devoted to an overview and history of window systems. While there is enough detail here to allow readers to write simple NeWS applications, the *NeWS Reference Manual* [SUN87a] should be consulted for a more complete treatment.

This book was written to refer to the NeWS 1.1 product, available from Sun and also available from several non-Sun suppliers. Shortly after this book is published, Sun will be releasing the next version of NeWS — the X11/NeWS merged window system. Chapter 10 is dedicated to an overview of that product, but X11/NeWS deserves a book of its own. All the code examples in this book have been tested on both NeWS and the X11/NeWS merge. Should there be another edition of this book, we will discuss some of the new development being done in the user interface tool-kit area on NeWS. Significantly, the NeWS Development Environment (NDE) is now being developed at Sun; NDE promises to eclipse existing user interface toolkit designs and window programming environments.

Before giving input on the many contributors to NeWS, the authors wish to give special thanks to John Warnock and Chuck Geschke of Adobe Systems. Without their design and implementation of the PostScript language, NeWS would not have been possible. The PostScript language is the future of printers and screens everywhere, and Adobe deserves the credit for teaching computer users the value of quality imaging in the everyday world.

Many people deserve the credit for this book, and for making NeWS a product. In the Sun window systems and user interface groups, the list of contributors is long. Credit is due to Tony Hoeber for the excellent *NeWS*

Technical Overview[SUN87b], to which this book owes much. Robin Schaufler's X11/NeWS paper[SCHA88], is the basis for all of Chapter 10. Craig Taylor built the first version of the NeWS interpreter with James; Jerry Farrell designed and implemented NeWS input handling; Owen Densmore single-handedly invented object-oriented, interactive programming in the PostScript language. Steve Evans and his windows platform team are the developers who have made NeWS and X11/NeWS a reality. We also acknowledge the Portable Windows Group, led by Steve Isaac, Amy Christen, and Steve Drach, as key contributors to the NeWS program and success. Warren Teitelman, Eric Schmidt, and Jim Davis provided critical management support and encouragement.

Our particular thanks go to our external contributors for Chapter 9. Martin Levy and Marty Picco from Parallax are the authors of the Parallax section. Mark Callow authored the Silicon Graphics contribution, and returned excellent feedback as a reviewer of several drafts. Mark and Silicon Graphics, as our first portable NeWS customer, returned extremely valuable feedback, which has improved the quality and design of today's product. Maurice Balick was responsible for the section on the NeWS OS/2 port done by Architech. Colleagues from SGI who contributed to Mark's paper were Peter Broadwell, Kipp Hickmann, Allen Leinwand, Rob Myers, Michael Toy and Glen Williams. Maurice was ably aided by Anthony Flynn, Marie B. Raimbault, Eddie Currie, and Sun's Portable NeWS group.

Our patient reviewers deserve high acclaim for wading through pages of code and syntax. S. Page deserves limitless credit for his tireless and incomparable editing skills, as well as his knowledge of NeWS. Henry McGilton gave us the benefit of his experience in writing and editing by his detailed notes and commentary. Brian Raymor, Martha Zimet, Steve Evans, Don Hopkins, Raphael Bracho, Sue Abu-Hakim, John Gilmore, Francesca Freedman and Tim Niblett all spent time and energy giving us comments and support.

Finally, we are grateful to Mark Hall and Gerhard Rossbach for making the book happen.

NeWS has been, and continues to be, a lot of fun. The interest and enthusiasm of the many NeWS supporters and developers has made it all worthwhile: our last thanks to you.

Table of Contents

Sun Technical Reference Library

1
Introduction

> *"If you ask the computer to help fix your broken lawnmower in the language that comes naturally to you, by typing in,* My lawnmower won't start. Can you help me fix it?*, the computer will respond with the same error message it would use if you had asked it to help you create a good recipe for sweet-and-sour pork:* WHAT ?*"*
>
> The Cognitive Computer

1.1 The Computer as a Means, not an End

Imagine that you are a university student, viewing a chemistry textbook in a window on a computer screen. There is an explanation of a certain molecule, with an accompanying picture. Using the mouse, you point at the molecule and rotate it slightly, then expand it, for a better view. Now you open up another window, containing your physics text. There is a description of an experiment with a ball being dropped from a tower, with an illustration. You push a button on the screen with your mouse, and the experiment is depicted on the screen. Push another button and you see a control panel that allows you to alter various parameters of the experiment, changing the gravity, height of the tower, density of the ball, and so on.

You are working on an inexpensive workstation in your dorm room, and the programs implementing these interactive textbooks are actually running on supercomputers located across campus, across the country, or even across the world.

In another scenario, you are collaborating with a Japanese colleague to develop a seminar series. She calls. Her video image appears in a window on your screen. She sends you a copy of the invitation being designed for the seminar: a window opens on your screen, displaying the invitation as you speak. The invitation appears, changes its user interface style and fonts. It adjusts for input devices from the original vertical text layout, Kanji, and Kanji tablet, to a horizontal layout, Roman, and three-button mouse. You insert your changes — sketching in alterations, changing words — and they appear dynamically on your colleague's screen (in the appropriate language and user interface style) as you discuss them.

2

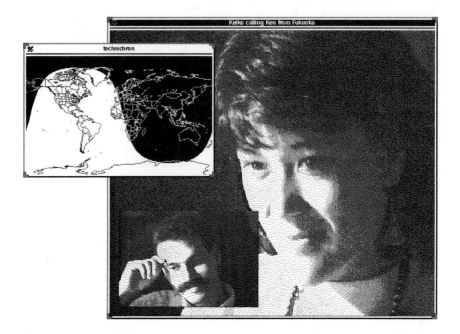

Figure: 1.1. Colleagues communicating between Japanese and English environments with the aid of video and graphic windows.

These two examples illustrate the changing role of the computer as a
tool. Today's window systems and user interfaces combine graphics, video,
and highly dynamic interaction to enhance the presentation and understanding of physical phenomena and to extend the capabilities of typical human
interaction. In the first scenario, the computer is acting as a window onto a
simulated natural world. Laws of interaction, representation, and reaction
are shown in three dimensions; light and color are represented realistically,
and in real time. Rather than extrapolating reality from a simulation, the
user sees "artificial reality" projected through the medium of his computer.
The second example shows the computer as an intelligent communicator,
transcending distance and culture and enhancing human interaction. Information flows through a computer "filter" and is transformed for the
destination environment and user. Both examples assume the constant pres-
ence of an unseen, powerful computer network.

In many ways, the examples above are glimpses of the functions of computers today. The computer workstation, with its high-resolution screen,
windows, and graphical capabilities, can realize these scenarios when
coupled with high-bandwidth networks. The decreasing price of computer
power and memory is making the power of a computer workstation accessible to the everyday business user and the university student, as well as to
technical professionals in every discipline. This power continues to increase

rapidly, while the costs to the computer user remain constant or decline.

Although the hardware capability is there, the software capability is lagging. The process of building software that enhances productivity without introducing complexity continues to be ill-understood, especially when coupled with the variety and breadth of existing computer environments. Computer networks complicate the problem. Networking is now the rule, rather than the exception, yet the development of high-performance, distributed applications across varied networks is still an art, not a science.

Our use of computers has changed dramatically since their inception. We have made the transition from machine language, paper tape, and computer-research facilities, to the world of the video game, home computer, and consumer goods based on the embedded microchip. Fourteen million personal computers were bought worldwide in 1987; ten million in the United States alone.[1] This proliferation of computers has taken place not only because of technological advances in speed, size, and manufacturing of the components, but also because our assumptions about interacting with computers have fundamentally changed. Prospective computer users in the past took it for granted that they would spend years learning specialized skills. Access to computers was limited to a dedicated few. Today, application developers and end-users are demanding that the computer learn to understand them, even to the point of being able to think and react like a human being. Computers are a means to attain an end, not as an end in themselves.

The typical computer user is no longer a computer expert, but the "naive" common person. This type of user demands an intuitive, consistent, and simple user interface. Increasingly powerful applications are required, forcing application developers to construct software capable of adapting to user preferences, languages, interface devices, and machine capabilities. Ease of use for the end-user, and ease of development for the application designer, are now expected system capabilities.

Here lies the domain of the window system.

1.2   Window Systems

Window systems have brought significant advances in mapping computer interaction to a model of human thought processes. Windowed displays show multiple applications at the same time, which fits with the human capability of thinking about several things at once. Visual user interfaces, with their menus, icons, and other graphical objects, are easier for users to learn, use, and remember. Window systems are a young technology: the trade-offs between simplicity and flexibility, the ability to make efficient use of computer networks, the integration of text and realistic graphics, and the minimization of the application development effort continue to be major design issues.

---

1. International Data Corporation, January 1989.

1.2.1   Simplicity versus Flexibility

There is a natural conflict between simplicity and flexibility in window system design. Everyone wants it simple. But simplicity for one person may be inordinately complex for another. The relative nature of simplicity puts the burden on flexibility. How flexible should the window system be?

How does flexibility impact the individual end-user? Scrollbars on the left-hand side, rather than the right, may be more convenient for a left-handed end-user. Near-sighted users want large default fonts. CAD users prefer a cross-hair cursor to a moving arrow. Some may want their screen to look like the factory floor machine it operates, others may want it to mimic the board at the stock exchange; standard menus and toggles will not serve their needs.

How does flexibility impact the application developer? Special window system primitives may dramatically increase the performance of their applications. Corporate standards may dictate the "look and feel" of a corporation's applications. How can such companies change the appearance and behavior of menus, panels, and buttons without decreasing application portability? Internationalized applications require different input devices and language support. Can the window system take care of these adaptations for the developer?

The window system framework must be capable of adapting to both anticipated and unanticipated change. Today's new user interface technologies are video, sound, gestures and eye tracking. Tomorrow's are unknown, but can we plan for their integration? Simplicity and flexibility combine to make both user and programmer interfaces more accessible to a larger group of people. However, physical, cultural, and application-specific differences, and varying preferences between people strongly influence learning and interaction techniques. The window system must reconcile these goals.

1.2.2   Networking

Networking and window systems are not generally related in users minds. As more computers are connected via low or high bandwidth networks, applications begin to share resources across a network. Window systems must support the development of these distributed applications. Simulations running on a supercomputer can display graphic output on, and receive user input from, a PC or workstation connected through a network. Co-workers may be updating the same diagram on their separate computer screens, while the software maintaining that diagram is resident on a third computer. Group development means that throughput, interactive response, data compression, and the ability to support different computer, software, and network architectures in such interconnected computers are important factors in the success of a window system in a networked environment.

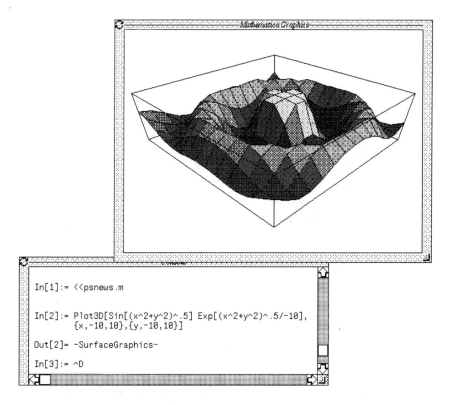

```
In[1]:= <<psnews.m

In[2]:= Plot3D[Sin[(x^2+y^2)^.5] Exp[(x^2+y^2)^.5/-10],
        {x,-10,10},{y,-10,10}]

Out[2]= -SurfaceGraphics-

In[3]:= ^D
```

Figure: 1.2.   Mathematica is a networked windowed applications that can be
distributed between NeWS workstations and supercomputers.

1.2.3   Sophisticated Graphics

Integration of text and high quality graphics has been a familiar problem
to graphic artists, but an unfamiliar concept to many computer applications.
In the past, most applications were limited to the output of simple text,
displayed on character-based terminals. Graphics, if any, were composed of
dashes, stars, or similar symbolic characters in a glowing green. The ASCII
encoding convention, which assigns a standard code to each of a limited set
of symbols, was (and still is) used to send character codes to the terminal,
which translated them directly into the pixels of the fixed character shapes
displayed on the screen.

Today, applications demand the equivalent output of the graphic artist's
brush: continuous, complex curves, color, shading, and dimension. Text
must have the same flexibility as graphics: rotated, shaded, multiple styles,
and multi-dimensional. Scanned images bring photographs and printed

matter to the screen; these imported images should be manipulated as easily as computer-generated graphics. Equivalently, computer-generated graphics should "look as good as the technology allows" wherever it is displayed,

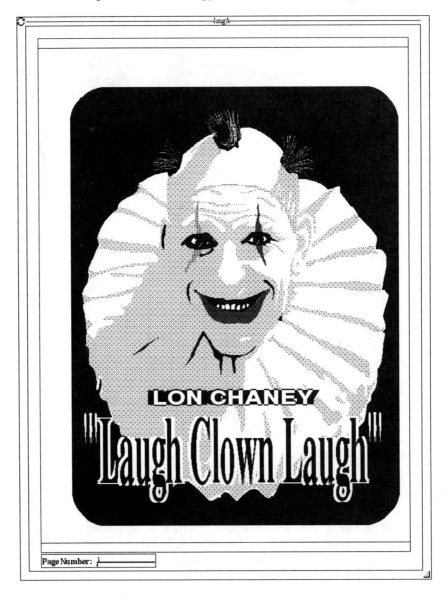

Figure: 1.3. Sophisticated graphic design represented in PostScript and viewed in a NeWS window.

on screen or on paper. Computer-generated forms should be accurately transformed to the printed page while taking also advantage of the superior resolution, shading, or color capabilities of the printed media.

1.2.4   Application Portability

Application developers are often faced with the problem of delivering a product on computer systems supplied by more than one vendor. The software development effort to support several computer platforms varies directly with the level of independence from the vendor that the developer can maintain. Application developers suffer because the window systems and operating systems supplied on these varying platforms differ. Window systems can also depend on hardware, such as the type of graphics device being used, or even the CPU architecture, which in turn further decreases the portability of the application from one computer system to another. The drive to minimize engineering development time has encouraged application developers to demand standard, device-independent, window systems on multiple platforms.

1.2.5   What is Needed?

Today, window-based applications lack the power and capability exhibited in the scenarios described at the opening of this chapter. New paradigms and techniques are needed. One of the elements required is a high-level graphics model or imaging model capable of representing text, graphical shapes, and images in a uniform, realistic, and device-independent way. Such an imaging model is only one part of the picture — it must be integrated with a window system capable of taking advantage of a heterogeneous computer network. The window system must be the medium for the molding of computer functions to user needs: applications must be able to adjust their appearance and interaction styles dynamically to conform to the special needs of the user, and the computer capabilities available. And, until the time when printers become obsolete through world-wide computer connectivity, an application should be able to display graphics on a printed page or within a window in exactly the same way, but not by adapting to the lowest common denominators of these and other mediums. Finally, the resulting technology should decrease the cost of developing software, and increase the the developer's ability to compete.

1.3   New Paradigms in Windows and Graphics

In the 1970s, researchers at Xerox Palo Alto Research Center developed a powerful new model for describing images. In 1982, two of these researchers, Charles Geschke and John Warnock, formed Adobe Systems and developed a page-description language based on this model. The language was introduced in 1984 under the name PostScript. The PostScript language is a high level programming language with powerful graphics primitives.

At the same time, researchers at Stanford, Carnegie-Mellon, and MIT began investigating a new approach to window systems: the *window server*, also referred to as a *network-based* window system. Window servers allow application programs running on one machine to use windows on another machine's display. Two window servers were built, the Andrew window system at Carnegie-Mellon, and the X window system at MIT, demonstrating the feasibility of window servers.

In October 1986, Sun Microsystems announced NeWS (Network/extensible Window System), a synthesis of the window server and page-description language technologies. NeWS makes the device-independent, powerful imaging model of the PostScript language available in a distributed window system. A key innovation is the use of the PostScript language, together with NeWS extensions, as a window system extension language, which makes possible a new level of interactive performance and flexibility. NeWS provides a platform, independent of hardware and operating system, on which highly diverse window applications and user interfaces can be built. NeWS applications attain an unprecedented level of visual quality, and exploit a coherency of network design new to window-based applications.

1.4   Book Outline

In keeping with the philosophy of NeWS, the chapter sequence of the NeWS Book is only intended to be a suggestion for reading order. Experienced developers may choose to avoid the preliminary chapters in which the basics of NeWS, window systems terminology and comparisons, and the PostScript language are discussed. Less knowledgeable readers may find the chapters discussing NeWS internals too detailed. The porting chapter should be of interest to all readers; outside contributors from Silicon Graphics, Architech, and Parallax describe interesting NeWS-based products. For detailed programming information, the *NeWS Manual* [SUN87a] should be consulted.

Chapter 2 gives some background and motivation to the development of NeWS, and describes its basic design.

Chapter 3 outlines what a window system actually is, and how its layers interact. This description will be useful not only to readers who have little experience with these systems, but also to experienced developers, who want to understand the terminology used throughout the book. In addition, the chapter examines several historically important window systems.

Chapter 4 offers an overview of the PostScript language, as defined by Adobe Systems, with an emphasis on the areas that are of particular importance to NeWS.

The additional NeWS facilities created specifically for an interactive window system environment are described in Chapter 5. These elevate NeWS as a PostScript language interpreter for the screen above PostScript language interpreters for printers. Input events, multiple overlapping drawing surfaces (or *canvases*), and *lightweight processes* are among the NeWS facilities available to the window system programmer.

Chapter 6 gives guidelines for programming the NeWS server by providing examples of functions and facilities which have been implemented inside the server. NeWS provides mechanisms to encourage object-oriented, class-based programming. The "Lite" toolkit is a user interface toolkit based on these concepts. It has been used as the basis for several applications on NeWS, and is described in detail.

Chapter 7 gives an overview of NeWS as a programming environment for developing distributed window-based applications. The chapter describes the responsibilities of a NeWS application and the NeWS server separated by a network, concentrating on applications written in the C language.

Chapter 8 gives a tour through a NeWS application, and outlines some of the techniques used to achieve good application performance

Chapter 9 briefly describes the steps that must be taken to port NeWS to different hardware, framebuffer, and operating system architectures. This chapter is mainly composed of three case histories of innovative NeWS ports by NeWS licensees. Parallax Graphics, Inc, has ported NeWS to a display board which has the capability to display live video. Silicon Graphics, Inc., did an early port of NeWS to a high-powered graphics workstation. Architech Corporation has recently released a port of NeWS to the OS/2 operating system environment.

Chapter 10 introduces the X11/NeWS merged window system. It describes the design of this merged window system, and explores some of the architectural issues that emerged during its design and implementation.

2
NeWS Overview

"A floor so cunningly laid that no matter where you stood it was always under your feet."

Spike Milligan and Eric Sykes

2.1   History

NeWS originated as a research project in 1984 at Sun Microsystems by James Gosling, later joined by David Rosenthal: the authors of the Andrew window system at Carnegie-Mellon University. NeWS, or SunDEW (Sun Distributed Extensible Windows), as it was originally called, arose out of an effort to examine some of the window system issues that both Andrew and the newly emerging X Window System explored, without product development constraints. What started as speculative research eventually developed into a product, and all of the normal constraints emerged, but not too early for NeWS to become an example of revolutionary window system design.

2.2   The Design

NeWS runs on a machine with one or more bitmapped displays. NeWS is designed to be portable between different computer systems and operating systems. It runs on machines ranging from a low-cost machine, such as an Atari or Amiga, to workstations based on powerful RISC architectures incorporating specialized graphics processors such as those from Sun and Silicon Graphics. NeWS acts as a *window server*, managing input and output on its host machine. Application programs — called *clients* — send messages causing NeWS to render images on the display. The clients may reside anywhere on the network. Server-based window systems are often called *distributed* window systems or *network* window systems because the server and its clients may be distributed over the network. Figure 2.1 shows one possible scenario in which the NeWS server, running on a workstation, serves a remote client running on a specialized machine. Window servers are often contrasted with *kernel-based* window systems, which are closely integrated into the operating system on a specific computer system. ("Kernel"

12

is frequently used as a synonym for the core of the UNIX operating system). Kernel-based window systems do not allow the distribution of window-based clients across the network; they have been the most common window system architecture until only recently. Chapter 3 discusses the evolution of window servers from the kernel-based window architecture.

The term window server is appropriate, but may have misleading connotations. When people hear the word server they tend to think of a piece of hardware in an air-conditioned room that supplies files or high-speed computation. Users of these resources are at other machines that are connected to the server via a network. In contrast, a window server supplies access to the display and the window system on its machine to other, connected machines across the network. However, the location of the window server with respect to the user is reversed: the server runs on the user's machine, and the clients run either locally or on remote (display-bearing or non display-bearing) machines.

NeWS is based on a novel type of interprocess communication. Interprocess communication is usually accomplished by sending messages from one process to another via some communication medium. Messages are usually a stream of commands and parameters. One can view these streams of commands as a program in a very simple language. NeWS extends this to be a general-purpose programming language. Programs then communicate by sending programs that are interpreted by the receiver. This process has profound effects on data compression, performance, and flexibility.

The PostScript programming language, as defined by Warnock and Geschke at Adobe Systems, is used in this way as a communication mechanism for printers. The PostScript language was conceived as a way to communicate with a printer. Computers transmit PostScript programs to the printer; these are then interpreted by a processor in the printer, and this interpretation causes an image to appear on the page. The ability to define functions allows the user to extend and alter the capabilities of the printer.

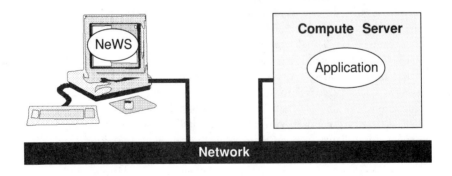

Figure: 2.1.   Application running on a compute server, with NeWS running on a workstation.

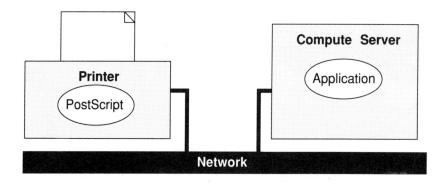

Figure: 2.2.   Application sending a PostScript program to a printer, in order to get
a document printed.

This extension model has powerful implications within the context of
window systems. It provides a graceful way to make the system more flexible. It also offers elegant solutions to performance and synchronization
problems. For example, in drawing a grid, you do not transmit a large set
of lines to the window system, you merely send a program containing a
loop of commands. The client's ability to send a program either locally or
over the network to execute within the NeWS server is referred to as *downloading*. The client's ability to download programs into the NeWS server
makes it possible to execute complex tasks simply and quickly.

NeWS uses the PostScript language as a window system extension
language. The PostScript language turns out to have been an excellent
choice. It is a simple, well-structured language, has a well-designed
graphics model, and it is compatible with many of today's printers due to
the wide acceptance of the PostScript page description language as a standard.

NeWS is structured as a server process that contains many *lightweight
processes* (discussed in Chapter 5). These processes execute PostScript programs. Client programs talk to NeWS through byte streams. Each of these
streams generally has a lightweight process associated with it. Messages
pass between client processes (running somewhere on the network) and the
processes resident within the NeWS server. These processes can perform
operations on the display and receive events from the keyboard and the
mouse. They can talk to other processes within NeWS that, say, implement
menu packages.

The NeWS server is centered around the PostScript language as an extension language. NeWS is a set of mechanisms. Policies are implemented as
replaceable NeWS procedures. For example, NeWS has no window-
placement policy. It has mechanisms for creating windows and placing them
on the screen, given coordinates for the window.

14

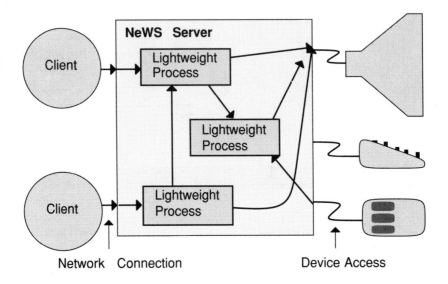

Figure: 2.3.   The NeWS server contains a number of lightweight PostScript pro-
                cesses that send messages amongst themselves and to Unix processes
                and devices. The messages sent from Unix processes (clients) are
                PostScript programs that are executed by the server.

The choice of those coordinates is up to some PostScript program within
NeWS. If a user or programmer wishes to modify the behavior of window
placement behavior, he has only to download a new window placement program into the NeWS server.

   In the context of this book, for readability and convenience, when we refer to PostScript programs running within NeWS, these programs and the
operators they use may include both standard PostScript graphics output
commands and NeWS interactive features structured on the PostScript
language model. Where the distinction is important, we will explicitly dif-
ferentiate NeWS functionality and PostScript language functionality.

2.3   Extensibility

   Extensibility in the context of a window system bears explanation. There
is great diversity in the extent of flexibility, or tailoring, permitted by different window systems. At one extreme are systems like Andrew,
MSWindows, and the Macintosh window system, where little can be
changed in either the user or programmer interface. In the middle are systems such as the X Window System, which has provisions for new menu
packages or new layout managers, but in which adding significant new

functionality to the window system (through the addition of new object libraries) is difficult to do in a way that is independent of the X server implementation. At the far end are open systems like Smalltalk, where it is simple for a skilled user to modify any part of the system's behavior. Some of these systems will be discussed in more detail in the next chapter.

To illustrate the differences in window system flexibility, consider what must be done to change the background grey pattern on the desktop. On the Macintosh this is easy because the designers included this option as a configuration choice. On the other hand, changing the behavior of the up/down buttons in the scrollbar is impossible. Andrew's background grey is not a configuration option; it cannot be changed without editing and re-compiling the source code for the window server, an option that is not available to ordinary users. Smalltalk makes it fairly easy since the component of the window system that deals with the background grey is small and well-contained, as is the component that deals with scrollbars, and it can be replaced incrementally without disturbing surrounding modules. The general difficulty is finding out which piece to replace and how it is specified. Smalltalk systems generally have the full source code available along with a powerful browsing facility: this makes the task possible and easy, but only for a skilled developer, not the general end-user.

NeWS tries to supply an extremely high level of flexibility to both the end-user and the programmer. Two main features of NeWS contribute to its extensibility. First, the PostScript language is an interpreted programming language that permits the definition of new functions. Second, the NeWS architecture allows clients to place PostScript code into the window server at any time, even while the server is running. Together these features let clients program the window server to meet their specific needs. Instead of requesting the server to perform functions on their behalf, NeWS clients pass the server code to execute.

2.4 Simplicity of User and Programmer Interface

Window systems have a wide range of complexity in their user interfaces, such as how menu title bars are drawn, and whether or not the user can stretch a window by clicking the left button in the upper right hand corner of the window outline. Some, like the Macintosh, or the OPEN LOOK user interface, have simple and consistent user interfaces that are easy for novices to learn. The Andrew window system has a very simple style that is easy to teach, use, and document. But Andrew's simplicity comes at the cost of rigidity, or loss of flexibility for the user that wishes to change the user interface. In some window systems, experienced users find the help and menu interaction cumbersome, while window systems tuned to expert needs are often too complex for novices. However, systems are rarely rigidly fixed at one of these extremes. They usually have accelerators for expert users and simple menu interfaces for novices.

NeWS makes no commitment to a particular user interface. It supplies general and powerful mechanisms that allow the builder of a user-interface toolkit or of an individual application to make the appropriate user-interface trade-offs. A window manager and user-interface toolkit is supplied with NeWS (described in Chapter 6); several window managers and user interface toolkits are available for X11/NeWS. Each of the NeWS-based window managers or toolkits can be modified or completely replaced by implementing appropriate procedures in the PostScript language.

Figure 2.4 illustrates how NeWS can support multiple user interfaces for an application, without any change being made to the application. Several copies of the application are started one after another. A new user interface package (a PostScript program, downloaded into the NeWS interpreter) replaces the existing user interface package between successive copies of the application. The look and feel of each copy varies — but the application is unchanged. In addition to supporting multiple user interface styles, NeWS can impose a global user interface on applications while the applications are running. This flexibility could allow end-users to determine the kind of user interface they prefer and apply that to all of the applications they purchase, without forcing the application developer to supply multiple user interfaces. Corporations can impose a corporate-wide user interface standard, or they may have their administrators use an MSWindows-style interface, while their engineers use an OPEN LOOK interface, and still permit them to interchange the same applications and the same set of hardware.

Trade-offs of simplicity and complexity are also found in the programmer interfaces to window systems. Simple interfaces often make unusual operations difficult. In the Andrew system, direct program manipulation of bitmaps is almost impossible, while in the SunWindows system it is impossible to avoid. Powerful programming interfaces tend to be complex, and can contain so much functionality that they are hard to learn and use, as well as to implement efficiently. This complexity is partly an inherent problem, and partly due to the tendency of systems to accrete features as they mature. The best compromise is an programming interface that can be learned and used incrementally. The developer can begin simply, and gradually progress to understand and use more complex functionality.

Because NeWS is based on an existing programming language and model, the issue of the programmer interface specification was to some extent avoided. The PostScript language has a simple, easy-to-understand design, in part because of the constraints of the original target environment (printers). The facilities NeWS adds for interaction and windows have been carefully specified to give a superset of PostScript language functionality, rather than conflict with the existing PostScript language constructs.

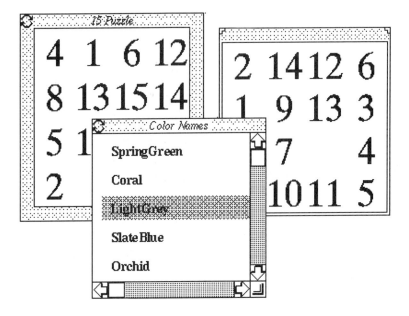

Figure: 2.4.   Several different window styles. These are implemented by packages dynamically downloaded into NeWS between instantiations of the programs.

Programming directly to NeWS (as opposed to programming to higher-level toolkit or application interfaces) involves writing and understanding PostScript programs. This is covered in Chapters 4-8.

2.5   Device Independence and Graphics Model

Window systems vary in their level of device independence. Many window systems are originally intended for a particular technological base, and the assumptions built into that base often creep into the higher levels of the design. When faced later with different technology, these assumptions can cause serious problems. A common one is the use of the *RasterOp* or *bitblt* graphics model (discussed in more detail in Chapter 3), which involves direct manipulation of blocks of individual pixels on the screen. While bit-blt works well with monochrome displays, it does not extend cleanly to color. Boolean combination functions between color pixel values do not make much sense. For instance, one often draws transient rubber band lines by XOR-ing them with the image. XOR-ing colormap indices 8 to 24 bits deep can lead to some pyrotechnic effects since the results have little logical meaning. Avoiding these effects requires careful control of pixel and colormap values.

Many window systems are initially built for a particular piece of hardware. Decisions tend to be made less in favor of what is "right" and more in favor of what fits in with the hardware at hand. A good example of this is the X10 window system, which began as a window system for VAXes with VS100 displays. The communication protocol between the X10 server and client programs is based on C structures, whose internal representation is very VAX-specific. VAX C structures do not map well to other machines: byte ordering, size, and field alignment differ from machine to machine. X10 has an imaging model that was determined by the microcode in the VS100, and it uses the VS100 font format. Unfortunately, the VS100 font format has some technical idiosyncrasies: for example, it isn't possible to draw a text string where adjacent characters overlap. This can be necessary, for example, when using an italic font. The "*i*" and "*j*" in the italic pair "*ij*" overlap. The keyboard support in X10 was entirely determined by the DEC LK201 keyboard, so that porting X10 to a machine with a different keyboard required emulation of the LK201. The next version of the X window system, X11, fixed all of these problems.

Andrew is a good example of a window system that was designed without a specific piece of hardware in mind. This result was an accident of the political situation during development: its intended hardware did not exist, had not even been designed and was conceived in relative isolation from the design of Andrew. Andrew emerged as a design for a black box. All that was known about the eventual system was that it would run Unix and that it would have a bitmap display. At the time, these constraints created a painful situation, but in retrospect they were a great blessing since they resulted in an extremely hardware-independent, portable window system.

The correct choice of a graphics model is crucial to achieving device independence. The more abstract the model, the more room there is for the underlying implementation to accommodate different technologies. Consider the representation of color. There are three common ways that color is available for display devices: 1-bit black and white (constant small set of colors); 8-bit color with a colormap (variable small set of colors); and 24-bit color (all possible colors available everywhere). Integrating these three implementations of color is a thorny but important problem. Most window systems support this by providing a different application programming interface to set color for every hardware implementation. This makes it difficult to write device-independent applications.

The choice of a graphics model is also critical to the graphics capabilities of a window system. Many systems provide only RasterOp, vector drawing, and simple text. On the other hand, systems such as the Macintosh, which has a much richer graphics model, have a flair for more graphically interesting applications. Richer models, however, are more difficult to implement and more difficult to understand, providing the window system developer with a difficult balancing act. The Macintosh is able to draw complex curves, scale images, and even clip scaled images to regions bounded by complex curves. Andrew, X10 and X11 lack these capabilities, or rather, they leave their implementation to the developer.

The NeWS graphics model is based on the stencil/paint model provided by the PostScript language. This graphics, or imaging model, is at a high enough level of abstraction to provide device independence along with a rich set of graphics capabilities to NeWS-based applications. Applications are not written in terms of specific hardware, therefore they need not be concerned about the resolution of the display, or whether the display is monochrome or color. Also, NeWS clients can automatically benefit from special high-performance graphics hardware, since the imaging model maps easily to many graphics accelerators. System vendors can provide acceleration through their NeWS server implementations while keeping the NeWS programming and graphics interfaces constant.

NeWS applications are even isolated from whether the output device is a printer or a display. Since NeWS contains a PostScript language interpreter similar to the one found in laser printers, a given series of PostScript language statements will render the same image whether sent to a NeWS window or to a printer containing a PostScript language interpreter. Thus, it is easy to preview printer output on the screen, or to send the contents of a window to the printer.

The two images in Figure 2.5 demonstrate the device-independent nature of the PostScript language. The image on the left was printed by sending a PostScript program directly to the printer; the one on the left is a snapshot of the same PostScript program rendered within a NeWS window.

2.6   Networking

In a distributed networked environment, accessing windows on another machine should be as natural as transparently accessing remote files via Sun's Network File System (NFS). Workstations and, increasingly, personal computers, are best used as elements in a heterogeneous environment, communicating over a network with other machines ranging from low-cost terminals, through workstations, to supercomputers. NeWS puts the resources of such a distributed computing environment on the screen. NeWS client programs don't have to run on the computer with the screen; they may be distributed in different ways across both client and server machines depending upon the resources available and the usage of the network. Experiences with Andrew and X indicate that the flexibility of client program location is valuable both for good local performance and an efficient use of resources across the global network.

Real-time response over a network is difficult in a server-based window system since the server usually has to pass messages to the client and wait for a response from the client whenever input or output occurs requiring

Figure: 2.5.   The device independence of NeWS lets one image appear as output on
multiple devices, such as printers and monitors. Notice that because
the printer has a higher resolution than the display, the image rendered
by the printer is smoother.

action from the client. The first window server designs suffered from poor
performance in interactive applications because of a communications bottleneck. Hundreds of messages flowing back and forth in interactive

situations, such as dragging a slider, severely impacted performance.

NeWS eliminates this real-time bottleneck by using the PostScript language as its means of communication with clients. Clients, instead of making function calls, pass PostScript statements that are interpreted by the server. Since PostScript is a general programming language, it allows the use of repetitive programming constructs, such as loops, and permits client-specific information storage in data structures inside the NeWS server. Use of these features results in a denser encoding of client-specific information than with a fixed, non-programmatic protocol. More information can be passed to the server in a smaller number of messages, making better use of network bandwidth. In addition, since the client can pass arbitrary PostScript programs, critical functions requiring much updating of the display can be programmed into the server, eliminating much of the communication overhead between the client and the server.

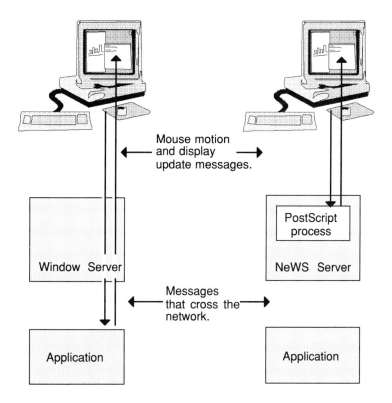

Figure: 2.6.   Network traffic when tracking the mouse. In the first scheme, messages get sent over the net every time the mouse moves. In the sceond, used by NeWS, the application has downloaded a piece of code that handles mouse events for it.

This gain from the elimination of network traffic overhead must be balanced against the loss inherent in using an interpreter. PostScript programs are generally slower than C programs. It is usually a mistake to do extensive calculation or build large elaborate data structures by programming in the PostScript language.

In Figure 2.6, an application is tracking the position of the mouse by redrawing a spline curve every time the mouse moves. Monitoring the mouse movements and repainting the spline is performed within the server by a procedure downloaded by the application. This rubber-band spline is not a necessary built-in function for a window system, but in NeWS applications (as in PostScript printers), an application can define new procedures.

2.7   Conclusion

This ubiquitous use of the PostScript language is a key feature of NeWS. The PostScript language gives NeWS two things that distinguish it from other window systems: an advanced imaging model and extensibility. NeWS brings the powerful industry-standard, and device-independent PostScript language imaging model to the display. NeWS dramatically expands the solution space available to developers. At any time, they can extend the capabilities of the server by defining new PostScript procedures. This extensibility of the system is key to NeWS functioning well in a distributed environment. Judicious use of this flexibility enhances performance, and allows client-specific protocols and data compression on the communication channel. The dynamic, interpretive server can act as the central authority for system behavior, or, can allow applications to define a unique environment.

3
Window System Architecture:
History, Terms and Concepts

"Architecture, in general, is frozen music."

Friedrich Von Schellig

3.1 Introduction

This chapter defines and explains the terms that commonly describe window systems. It establishes a general level of understanding for future chapters. The four parts of this chapter offer:

a layered model of window systems;

a historical survey of window systems, illustrating how a number of systems fit into the model;

a detailed review of the components of the layered model;

an examination of the relationship between window system architectures and their environments.

3.2 Anatomy of a Window System

The study of window systems is an emerging discipline, so terminology is not well-defined. There is a model of the window system that has six layers spanning the application to the hardware. Higher layers are closer to the application, and, ultimately the user. Lower layers correspond to primitive functions, finally ending in hardware components.

We will cover four layers of the model: the User Interface Toolkit, Window Manager, Base Window System, and Imaging/Graphics library.

Two confusing terms are *Base Window System* and *Window Manager*. They are sometimes used interchangeably or are used with a broader scope. In this book we use *window manager* to mean the part of the total window architecture that deals with the user interface to windows: the borders around them, the user commands to open, close, and move them around.

24

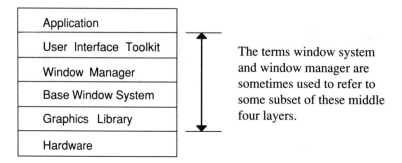

The terms window system and window manager are sometimes used to refer to some subset of these middle four layers.

Figure: 3.1.   Four layers of the window system lie between applications and hardware.

We use *base window system* to mean the part of the architecture that deals with resource allocation, synchronization, communication between graphics and higher levels, and input distribution. We use *window system* to refer to some subset of these four layers. The NeWS window system consists of the bottom two of the four layers; while the Macintosh window system (the "Mac ROM") consists of all four layers

This layered window system model is useful, but it will break down in some areas: today's window systems have often grown "organically" rather than in a strictly modular way. However, it does show one reason why comparisons between window systems can be confusing; they differ dramatically in the number of layers they implement.

Note that the operating system is not included as a layer in our model; this is because there are several ways in which the operating system can interact with the window system. NeWS, and most other emerging window systems are network- or server-based, which implies that they have the status of a user-level process, and are not built into the operating system. Until recently, most window systems have been kernel-based, or built into the operating system core, or *kernel*. The following sections discuss several examples of both types of window system architectures.

3.3   A Brief History of Window Systems

For the moment, you will have to take the model on trust. We will cover each of the layers in detail later. We now make a brief historical survey of window systems to see how each fits into the layered model.

3.3.1 Smalltalk

Smalltalk is the common ancestor of all window systems [GOLD83]. It was produced at Xerox PARC in the early 1970's. Initially implemented on the Alto[THAC88], a small machine with only 64K of memory, there have been many subsequent implementations. The first practical one was on the Dorado-class machine.

Smalltalk is a complete universe. It includes an operating system, a language, a window system, and a variety of other tools. In the first versions of Smalltalk the operating system was indistinguishable from the window system. It all fit together in one address space on the bare machine. In later implementations Smalltalk was still a complete universe, but it was usually layered on top of an operating system.

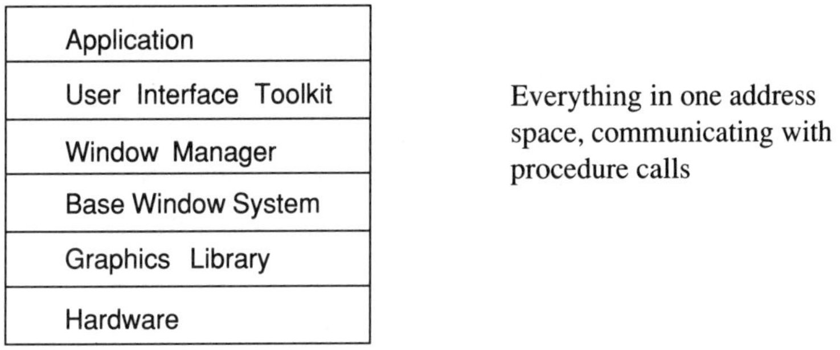

Application
User Interface Toolkit
Window Manager
Base Window System
Graphics Library
Hardware

Everything in one address space, communicating with procedure calls

Figure: 3.2.   The single address space, single process structure of Smalltalk.

This single-process, single address space structure leads to the simplest window system architecture. There are few operating system problems. One process has complete control and total access to the system. It has no need, for example, to arbitrate among multiple processes for access to a display processor. There is only one monolithic process.

The simplicity of systems like Smalltalk is their biggest limitation:

Users want to be able to perform multiple tasks concurrently: read mail, work on a document, and use other applications, all at the same time. In a single process environment, these different applications have to be fused together into one program. In some cases, tricks such as DOS's "terminate and stay resident" can be used to stitch together disparate applications, but these are only suitable for small desktop accessories.

Because there is one address space, an application with a bug in it can "crash" not just itself, but the entire computer system.

These simple systems normally lack virtual memory. Without it, there is a
fixed limit on how large an application can grow, thereby limiting the
application functionality.

The Smalltalk language is based on *object-oriented programming*. It uses
classes to define the properties of *objects* that are operated on by *methods*.
The computer system is protected from crashes, even though everything is in
one address space, by linguistic controls that limit the damage that can be
caused by an errant program. These controls are possible because there is
only one language. One nice side effect of this makes Smalltalk the ultimate
in flexible systems. It provides a *code browser* that gives users access to
all the code of the entire system. Using the browser, the user can replace
any part of the system on-the-fly.

The Smalltalk graphics model is not very sophisticated. It was designed
for monochrome bitmap displays and was intended for text/terminal applications and not for graphics. Everything was centered around the RasterOp
graphics model: Smalltalk dealt strictly with lines, rectangles and text.
Since early versions only implemented rectangular clipping, they could only
draw in the uppermost window. The language was the focus, graphics was a
relatively minor consideration and portability was not a design goal.

The base window system in Smalltalk was very simple. It was implemented using Smalltalk's class mechanism. Because there was only one
address space and only one process, there were no synchronization or communication problems. The window manager was structurally intertwined with
the base window system.

The Smalltalk user interface broke a lot of new ground, introducing windows, scrolling, pop-up menus, and the virtual desktop.

The toolkit level included a modeless editor that used cut-and-paste and
pop-up scrollbars. It introduced the Model/View/Controller (MVC)
paradigm, breaking up the user interface implementation into three components. This division is still used by most modern toolkits. These are:

the *model*, which describes an application data structure, like a text file
   or a drawing.

the *view*, which describes how that data structure maps onto the
   display surface.

the *controller*, which describes how input events alter the model and view.

The MVC paradigm is used in the example program of Chapter 8.

3.3.2   DLisp

DLisp was a version of Lisp developed in 1977 at PARC. PARC engineers had a problem. They had small and underpowered Altos which could do graphics, and they had a big PDP-10 that could run Lisp. So they built *Display Lisp*, or DLisp, which used a Lisp system on the PDP-10 that was extended to communicate over the Ethernet to an Alto. This was the first network window system. Like Smalltalk, DLisp was a one language, one address space window system, although it did break new ground in developing network communications. In time DLisp was superseded by Interlisp-D. It disappeared and is generally unknown.

The DLisp "graphics server" ran on the Alto (it was the only thing running on the Alto). The server depended upon a very low-level graphics model that was essentially identical to Smalltalk's. It supported only RasterOp, lines and text. One big advance over Smalltalk's graphics model was that it implemented complicated clipping, allowing graphics operations to be performed on windows other than the one on top. It also supported the use of multiple fonts, which didn't come until later in Smalltalk.

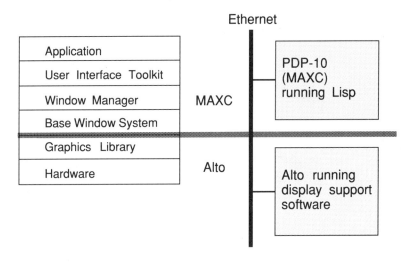

Figure: 3.3.   DLisp came in two parts; the lower levels on the Alto and the higher levels on the PDP-10.

The rest of the DLisp system ran on the PDP-10 and contained most of the window system, the user interface toolkit and the application. The PDP-10 communicated across the Ethernet with the Alto using a custom protocol. Like Smalltalk, it was an experimental testbed: graphics were a minor consideration.

The DLisp user interface was implemented on the PDP-10; the Alto merely performed graphics. The entire DLisp system was limited by communication performance constraints. Network round-trip times made changing cursor shape and dragging images too slow, so these operations were not supported by the base window system on the PDP-10. The user interface had a multiple desktop scheme that was eventually abandoned, after the developers decided that icons were a much better idea. DLisp introduced another interesting, but aborted, concept: windows "faded away" if not used by the user for a period of time.

DLisp placed the window system in a user-level process. This structure eases window system development and protects the computer system against accidental or malicious destruction of internal data. The window system is much easier to maintain and enhance as a user-level process, rather than as part of the operating system kernel.

3.3.3 The Mesa Systems

After DLisp, Xerox PARC developed a number of window systems supporting multiple processes in a single address space[LAMP88]. These were all implemented in the Mesa programming language.

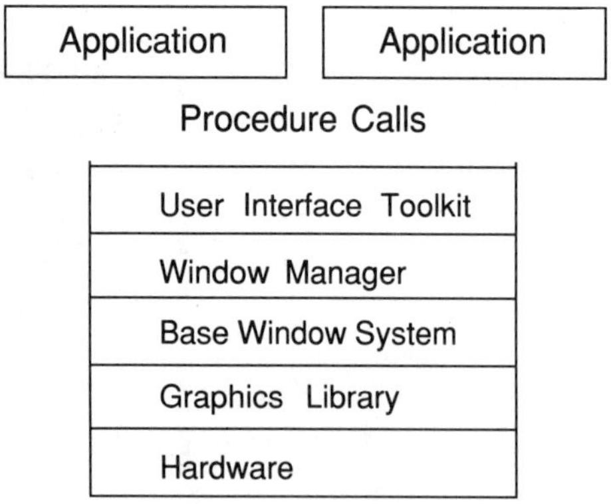

Figure: 3.4.   Mesa supported multiple processes in a single address space.

When a single address space environment has multiple processes, concurrent applications like the two in figure 3.4 become possible. Multiple concurrent applications introduce two problems: *synchronization* and *protection:*

The synchronization problem arises when client processes, running in parallel, invoke the window system to manipulate windows and perform graphic operations in them. As an example, the user sitting at the workstation performs an operation that causes a window to move, and the movement takes place while the client processes draw in their windows. A process whose window becomes partially obscured can find itself halfway through drawing a line with a window that is no longer in the same place, or into a window that is not the same shape as when the process was started. Drawing the line and moving the window must be synchronized to avoid collisions of this type.

The protection problem is common to both the single-address-space, multiple-process and the single-address-space, single-process model described earlier. One misbehaving program can bring down the computer system by manipulating the window system's structures. In a multi-process system, one program can also destroy all of the programs, as well as the window system, unless there is some protection mechanism or set of conventions that all programs follow. This can lead to a very fragile system, where one bug in one program can drag everything down.

At PARC, both the synchronization and protection problems were solved using the facilities of the Mesa and Cedar/Mesa languages and the Pilot operating system. They have very good synchronization facilities, and guarantee that programs do not randomly destroy memory belonging to other programs. This guarantee can be made because Mesa and Pilot check array bounds and restrict the operations allowed on pointers. Many Lisp machines deal with the protection problem in the same way.

Some linguistically protected systems, such as Smalltalk, go further and do not support pointers at all. However, the urge to avoid protection is such that these implementations typically have loopholes to allow programmers to get around the language protection and manipulate pointers directly.

3.3.3.1   Tajo

Tajo (1977), another Mesa window system, was one of the first window systems to deal with multiple processes in a single address space, and it was the system that introduced icons. Tajo was also the first notification-based system. The "inner event dispatch loop" wasn't in the application, it was in the window system. An application didn't implement a main loop, it simply registered procedures to be called when events occurred. The window system was in control, simplifying the system, but confusing many programmers who were used to being in control.

3.3.3.2   Docs

Docs (1980) was another multiple processes, one address space window system implemented in Mesa under the Pilot operating system. One of its real innovations was that it supported an advanced imaging model based on a library known as "Cedar Graphics." It supported scaling and rotation, curves, images, and retained windows. The Cedar Graphics model evolved and eventually became the basis for both Interpress and PostScript, which are both languages for communicating with printers.

Like Smalltalk, Docs had an object-oriented toolkit based on the model/view/controller paradigm. But it went a step further and attempted to integrate documents into the toolkit. It defined a set of classes to implement documents. Documents had methods for presenting themselves in windows and they could contain subviews on other documents. There were many good ideas in Docs, but it was too slow to be useful. Not until the Andrew window system was an integrated document model implemented as a part of a toolkit that performed well enough to be generally used.

3.3.3.3   Star

Star (1981) was Xerox's attempt to transfer the technology developed at PARC to the market[LIPK82]. It retained the underlying window system technology, but introduced a number of concepts to the user interface. Among these were a consistent office model, with icons representing files (documents) and directories (file cabinets), a consistent selection paradigm for all visible objects, a consistent mechanism for altering the attributes of visible objects through property sheets, and an omni-present editor. Editing was not part of individual applications, it was a system-provided service.

3.3.3.4   Viewers

Viewers (1981) took a step backwards from Docs to regain the performance that Docs lost. Initially, it backed out of the Cedar Graphics model as being too expensive, but it was eventually reintroduced. From the Star system it picked up the notion of *tiling* windows on the screen. Windows could not overlap, but were laid out much like tiles on a wall.

3.3.4   NU

In 1981 at MIT, the advent of the Motorola 68000 led to an attempt to build a workstation and its software environment called NU. Jack Test built a simple window system entirely inside the UNIX kernel. It supported overlapping windows, each of which behaved like a conventional terminal.

The kernel is often a convenient place to put device support and a centralized synchronization point in the interests of performance. But there are problems placing anything into the operating system. The debugging tools are usually poor, and any bug that does escape detection threatens the integrity of the entire system. Development cannot proceed in parallel with other uses of the system. A large body of code is placed in memory, which makes that memory unusable by other processes, since the kernel is typically not paged (it is "wired-down").

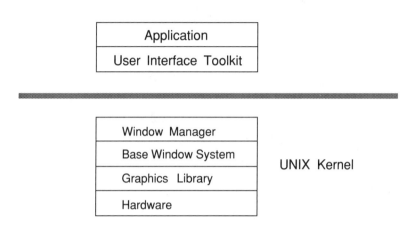

Figure: 3.5.   The NU window system was built in the UNIX operating system.

The limits on the code that can be installed in the operating system meant that the NU window system was too simple to be really successful. Its capabilities were limited to terminal emulation, and simple graphics. Its performance was limited by the fact that every window system operation was a system call.

3.3.5   SunWindows

In 1983 Steve Evans of Sun Microsystems produced SunWindows[SUN85]. It was the first widely used UNIX window system. As such, it was one of the first window systems to deal with the problems of multiple processes and multiple address spaces. Providing good performance for simple window operations, rather than fancy graphics, was the goal of the design. It is now a mature and stable system, but it is showing its age.

Like NU, its implementation was entwined with the UNIX kernel. But unlike NU, only a small part of the system resided there. The window hierarchy database was kept in the kernel, along with system calls to manipulate it and synchronization facilities to manage concurrent access. Each application had the graphics device mapped into its address space and accessed it directly — the actual device drivers were not in the kernel, they were in the applications.

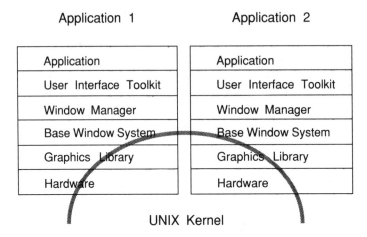

Application 1   Application 2

Figure: 3.6.   SunWindows is a multi-process, multi address-space system with synchronization in the UNIX kernel.

With each client having direct access to the display hardware, one would
expect excellent performance. When performance is worse than expected,
there are several possible reasons, including synchronization, and paging
overheads:

Clients that directly access the display hardware must synchronize among
themselves. It is usually impossible for two processes to be accessing the
device registers in parallel. For example, before drawing a line a client
must make sure that no other client is drawing lines and only when the
hardware is idle can it finally draw the line. Checking and locking can be
expensive, sometimes as expensive as a kernel call, and can dominate
the expense of drawing the line. The per-operation locking cost can be
reduced by increasing the granularity; instead of locking on every line,
lock before drawing a group of lines, and unlock afterwards. Unfortunately, putting the burden of choosing a suitable locking granularity on
the application programmer increases the chance for error.

If the hardware provides little support for graphics operations, as many
simple frame buffers do, then the graphics library that is replicated in
each client can become large. If there are many different display devices
and operations to be supported, the amount of replicated code can become
enormous. In systems with virtual memory, these large libraries can
cause substantial paging delays. If a large amount of code is being replicated and its sheer bulk is causing problems, attempting to keep it small
appears attractive. But this often involves exploiting fewer special cases
and avoiding other optimizations involving more speed at the cost of

more space. The effect of this replication is eliminated if the operating system supports shared libraries.

Aside from these performance issues, putting such a large body of code into each client process also introduces logistical problems for operating systems that do not support shared libraries:

It becomes much harder to make changes and fix bugs. Every client must be relinked to access the new routines. This applies even more to third-party software; it may take some time to get new libraries incorporated.

In this context, new display devices are, in effect, bugs. Because the device drivers are linked into the clients, introducing a new display type has the same problem as fixing a bug. Further, since an application has to contain drivers for every device it may encounter, it will be bigger than necessary.

The SunWindows approach also requires that client programs are "well-behaved." Checking and locking are not enforced by the window system. "Well-behaved" clients are expected to operate within the rules and use these protection protocols for the benefit of their fellow clients.

As one might expect, SunWindows was implemented in stages from the bottom up. The first releases provided only the base window system (SunWindows) and a window manager (SunTools). The graphics model was based on two libraries, Pixrects and Pixwins, implementing the Smalltalk RasterOp model.

As the technology advanced, SunWindows had to evolve to match, and this sometimes "broke" the low-level RasterOp model. With the introduction of color the uniform boolean operation model of RasterOp started to break down. Colormaps introduced another resource allocation problem. High performance accelerators demanded a higher level model that implemented more advanced features like curves, polygons, and 3D. The short term answer was to add device specific imaging models, but these caused porting problems for applications which needed to support multiple devices.

Since the SunWindows user interface was all in the application's address space, it was theoretically changeable. But in reality, the early system came without a toolkit, and the first toolkit was so complex that almost no one made any changes.

Eventually SunView, an object-oriented toolkit, was layered on the existing system, hiding most of their complexities and making the construction and modification of user interfaces much easier.

3.3.6 Andrew

Andrew (1983) was developed by two of the authors (Gosling and Rosenthal) at the Information Technology Center, a joint project of IBM and Carnegie-Mellon University[MORR86]. The goal of the project was to produce a workstation for the masses. In the beginning, the machine did not yet exist (it was to be the PC/RT), so Sun workstations were used as test-bed hardware. The center's goal was to produce applications for an educational environment. Producing a window system or toolkit was not a specific objective, except as needed for these applications. But neither a convenient window system or a toolkit was available at that time. These factors together led to a unusual set of goals:

The window system had to be portable and hardware independent. It was being written for a machine that was not yet designed.

It had to be simple and quick to implement so that real application development could begin as soon as possible.

It could not require changes to the UNIX kernel. The Sun operating system was distributed in binary form and the target system did not yet exist.

The solution was to implement the window system as a separate UNIX process. Applications communicated to this window server through UNIX sockets, using the TCP/IP protocol.

All window-related client requests are performed by sending messages to the server. With this scheme, all of the graphics and window management code is placed in one process: the window server. The window layout database, clipping regions, and all other relevant information is centralized, solving many of the organizational problems of the other window system architectures. In particular, the synchronization issue is solved by avoidance. The window system has only one thread of control and complete access to all information. Synchronization occurs by serializing the messages coming into the window system process.

The TCP/IP network protocol was used because it was the only available inter-process communication facility. It was expected to lead to poor performance, since communication between client and window system via message-passing can substantially increase the overhead of each operation.

The primary technique for achieving good network performance was batching, putting multiple client requests in each network packet. To make batching more useful, two additional things were done. Wherever possible, the requests did not return values, so that a round-trip between client and server was not required. Also, if a procedure did not return a value, then the call was not sent immediately, but was batched with successive requests. With a large enough message size and a protocol specification that

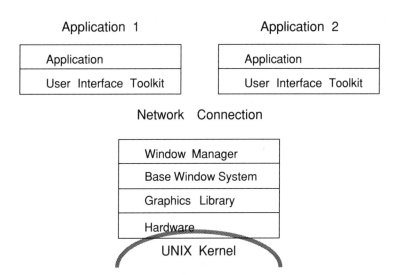

Figure: 3.7.   Andrew puts everything except the User Interface Toolkit in a user
level server process. Applications never see the hardware.

requires few replies, the per-message setup cost (delay, processing cost of
constructing a message, network usage) becomes insignificant.

The other important technique in Andrew was to maintain a low ratio of
bits passed in messages to bits altered on the screen and thereby reduce the
cost per pixel of message passing. Designing a protocol that operated at a
high level of abstraction lowered this critical cost. As an example, it is possible to design a protocol that allows only bitmaps to be sent to the
window system from the client. Thus, when a client wants to draw a text
string, all the bits for all the characters must be sent. In this case, the window system has a complete, simple model, but it will have poor
performance. On the other hand, if the protocol includes notions like
"font" and "string" then text can be shipped down in a very compact form.
The more that the window system understands at an abstract level, the
more efficient client-server communication will be.

Andrew was the first practical UNIX networked window server. It
demonstrated that server-based systems were possible. It also performed
well and, unexpectedly, proved that the ability to use window applications
across the network was very valuable. Furthermore, it was the first window system to be ported to a significant number of different workstations
and displays. Andrew was initially developed on a Sun-1 monochrome system and subsequently ported to a total of three CPU architectures and seven
display types: Sun-1 color and Sun-2 monochrome displays, monochrome
microVAXes, and PC/RTs with Vikings, APA-8s, and APA-16s.

As experience was gained, porting got easier. The fastest port ever was to the APA-16 display, which all told took three people less than four hours to complete!

Andrew has a RasterOp based imaging model, like so many other systems. However, its font model was quite sophisticated.

The window manager and the toolkit's menu package were in the server to provide a unified user interface and to increase performance. They were fixed, and it was impossible for an application to change them. Since one goal of the workstation was to enforce a consistent user interface, this limitation was acceptable. The window manager implemented a tiling window layout policy, which proved efficient and popular, but controversial.

The window system was designed in tandem with a toolkit supporting a high level document model, similar to Docs, which included a fancy WYSI-WYG text editor. Although the support for text was excellent, many of the applications showed the inadequacy of the graphics model.

In 1988, the Andrew toolkit, the applications, and the user interface style it was used to develop have been ported to the X11 window system.

3.3.7   The Macintosh

The Macintosh (1984) from Apple Computer was designed to be a system for the masses, a small machine with a high-quality user interface. It borrowed heavily from the Xerox systems — primarily Smalltalk, Star, and Tajo. The Mac was for users, not programmers. It was applauded for being easy to use, but it was initially condemned for being hard to program. Although it broke almost no new technical ground, it brought to the public a new way of dealing with computers and raised their level of expectation. It was a landmark in user interface design, proving that graphical interfaces were not just a neat idea, they had value in the market.

In many ways the Mac was a throwback, being a single address-space, single process machine with a very limited amount of memory. The various layers of the system were all intertwined. Since the market was end-users, not programmers, protection against buggy programs was not a large issue. Apple assumed that by the time users got the machine there would be no bugs. There really is no operating system on the Mac. The application is in charge. Everything else is a subroutine library.

The graphics model is one area where the Mac broke new ground. Quick-Draw[ESPI87], the graphics library, was based on the RasterOp model, but it added fancier fonts, curves, non-rectangular clipping, and regions. It was almost the first system that took graphical design seriously. Xerox's Star came earlier, but it didn't get the same exposure. As the Mac has evolved, it has shown strains of age analogous to SunWindows. For example, the initial color model was too simple and as hardware evolved the model had to be superseded.

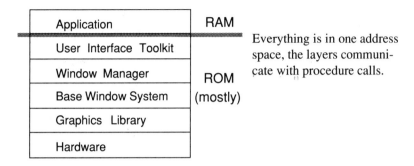

Application	RAM
User Interface Toolkit	
Window Manager	ROM
Base Window System	(mostly)
Graphics Library	
Hardware	

Everything is in one address space, the layers communicate with procedure calls.

Figure: 3.8.   The Macintosh is a single process, single address space system, with much of the window system in ROM.

The problems of the single-address-space/single-process operating system can be seen in their evolution — most are acquiring multiprocessing facilities. On the PC, Microsoft Windows and GEM added explicit support for multiple processes. On the Macintosh, the desk accessory mechanism, the Switcher, and the Multifinder are heading in the same direction. Unfortunately, multiprocessing is hard to graft onto a system once it is completed. Because it is so important, many applications will include their own limited form of multiple processes, and these private implementations will interfere with the way the evolving system wants to implement processes.

3.3.8   The X Window System

X (1985) began as the **W** (1982) window system, developed by Paul Asente and Brian Reid at Stanford University for the experimental V operating system. V was a high performance message passing system implemented on Sun hardware. In 1983 it was ported to VAXes and the VS100 display at the DEC Western Research Labs, but the slower message passing of UNIX made W's synchronous communication impractical. In the summer of 1984, Bob Schiefler and Jim Gettys at Project Athena, the IBM- and DEC- funded campus computing project at MIT, started work on a system based on asynchronous communication like Andrew, and called it X.

The first widely available version was X10[GETT86,SCHE86]. The architecture of X10 was almost identical to Andrew. Its major innovation was that the window management user interface was moved outside of the window system into a separate UNIX process.

Unlike Andrew, X10 made no attempt to impose a user interface. The user interface was provided by application libraries and special applications, such as the window manager. X10 gained flexibility at the expense of performance. Fortunately, it turned out that the performance cost was usually small. Like most network-based window systems, animated interactions in X10 (menus, rubber band lines) can lead to heavy network traffic when the server and application exchange messages each time that the mouse moves.

Since X10 was developed for VAXen with a VS100 display, the design gave little thought to portability. The VS100 was a relatively unsuccessful product and, even though MIT made the source code freely available, it is likely that X would have remained an obscure University system had it not been ported to more widely-available hardware. One of the most important of these early "public domain" X10 ports was undertaken over the Christmas 1985 holiday by two of the authors (Rosenthal and Gosling), who took the initial MIT source, ported it to the various Sun configurations, and returned the results to MIT for distribution. The fact that the system was freely available on a popular workstation like the Sun led to a rapid increase in interest and a number of other ports.

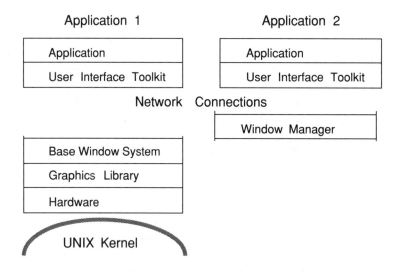

Figure: 3.9.   X10 was structured like Andrew, but the window manager was in a separate process.

X11 (1987) arose out of the efforts to fix some of X10's deficiencies. X10 had some major limitations, including an imaging model derived largely from the VS100's microcode, a font model ill-suited to supporting WYSIWYG editors, and several other VAX-specific features. So much in X10 needed fixing that compatibility had to be sacrificed. X11[SCHE87, SCHE88] was redesigned from a clean slate by a group of interested engineers, led by Bob Schiefler and including one of the authors (Rosenthal). One interesting aspect of X11 is that, unlike all the other systems mentioned in this chapter, a specification for it was written and intensively reviewed by electronic mail before anything was implemented. A group at DEC implemented a sample server based on this specification, and MIT distributed it to selected groups for alpha-testing. During these early phases, a joint effort between U. C. Berkeley and Sun made the first port of X11 (to Sun hardware), developed a portable color framebuffer driver, and produced a porting guide that enabled many other groups to get the sample server operational on their hardware.

Although the overall architecture of X11 is very similar to X10, the details are very different. In particular, portability and extensibility were major design goals.

Portability across displays was provided by defining six generic display types; applications are expected to adapt their behavior to whichever one of these types they use.

Extensibility was addressed by reserving a set of protocol op-codes. These op-codes can be used by code, linked into the server, implementing additional functions. Also, X11 provides support for managing the name-space of extensions, and an interface in the sample server to which extensions must conform to be regarded as portable[FISH87].

3.3.9   NeWS

The history of **NeWS** (1986) was covered in the previous chapter[GOSL86]. Fitting it into the layered model used in this chapter shows the flexibility it gains by having a protocol defined as a full progrmming language, which is then interpreted by a dynamic, extensible server. NeWS can be regarded as a a programming language environment — applications can interface to the system at any suitable level.

Applications can:

Be written entirely in PostScript, and reside in the single address-space, multiple process world of the NeWS server, seeing an environment similar to the Xerox PARC systems;

Access the system using raw PostScript imaging operators and NeWS input operators, seeing a system that looks much like the X11 window system, but with a more powerful imaging model;

Or access the system using a server-resident toolkit, seeing a system like Andrew with much higher-level operators, in which the network communication is in terms of objects such as menus and scrollbars.

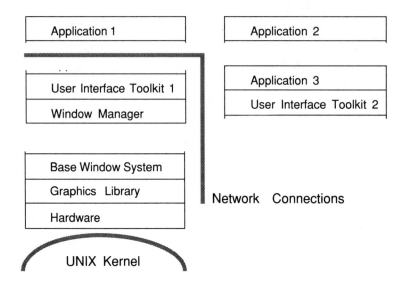

Figure: 3.10.   NeWS allows applications to access the server at various levels.

3.4   The Layers of the Window System Model

We now examine each of the layers of the model in turn, working from the application towards the hardware.

3.4.1   User Interface Toolkit

User interface toolkits have high-level tools which a window-application programmer can use to ease the development of a graphical user interface for an application. By encouraging the re-use of user interface components, toolkits establish uniformity among application user interfaces. A toolkit shields the application developer from having to know the underlying details of the window system architecture, yet offers the capabilities necessary for the design and implementation of a sophisticated user interface. Cursor control, window management, input handling, and clipping of graphical output are examples of low-level facilities that the toolkit hides from the application developer.

A toolkit normally provides:

a core that lays out user interface building blocks (sometimes called
   widgets) such as buttons and sliders, and handles input, routing it to
   the code implementing the appropriate widget.

a library of pre-defined widgets that can be attached to the core to provide a
complete user interface.

user interface prototyping tools, easing the process of attaching widgets to
the core.

The application developer forms the user interface with the prototyping
tools, selecting and positioning widgets from the library. The toolkit provides an application with the user interface look and feel determined by the
designers of the widget library. To change the look and feel, the widgets
must be changed. NeWS and its Lite toolkit, described in Chapter 6, are
unusual because they allow an application to dynamically change look and
feel without altering the implementation of the running application. In
most toolkits such changes can only be done by programming new widgets,
adding them to the library, and re-linking the application.

Most libraries offer widgets representing windows or frames, menus, and
control items (buttons, sliders, text fields, switches, meters, scrollbars,
and the like). When an instance of one of these components is attached to
the core, its location must be specified. Normally, a toolkit will provide
both for explicit positioning (put the record button at 200,160) and im-
plicit positioning (put the record button left of the stop button.)

Toolkits differ in the sophistication of the components in their widget
libraries. Some offer only simple components such as the buttons and sliders in Figure 3.11. Other libraries, like Andrew's in Figure 3.12, contain
very high-level application components such as text and graphic editors.
These powerful editors, allowing multiple fonts, formatting, cut-and-
paste, scrolling, and searching, are increasingly replacing character terminal
emulation as the major means of communication with applications, exploiting the interaction capabilities of the mouse and bitmap display to present
text in a denser yet highly readable form. A toolkit allowing an application
developer to use such editors as components has obvious advantages.

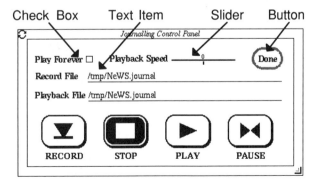

Figure: 3.11.   Toolkit components in a control panel.

With a mouse, a large display, multiple windows and powerful editors as the interface to applications, the ability to cut, copy and paste information between windows becomes increasingly important. In this area, the toolkit normally provides two things:

1   A consistent user interface, allowing the user to select part or all of the information displayed by a widget, and invoke transfer operations.

2   A programming interface between the source and destination widgets of a transfer operation, and the low-level *selection service* of the base window system, which actually transfers the information.

Toolkit normally support either the "clipboard" user interface style with operations like "Cut" (which moves information from a source widget to the clipboard), "Copy" (which copies information from a source widget to the clipboard), and Paste (which moves information from the clipboard to a destination widget), or the "selection" user interface style, (which transfers information directly between widgets without a clipboard-style intermediary.)

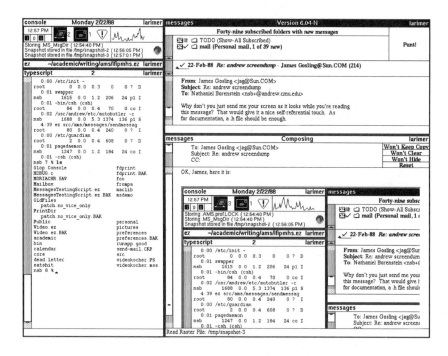

Figure: 3.12.   Andrew in action: performance monitors, a terminal emulator, and a mail session.

The programming interface to the base window system's selection service will normally provide only for the transfer of uninterpreted data. It is the source widget's responsibility to convert its internal data representation for the selected information into a form that the destination widget can understand in terms of *its* internal data representation.

Toolkit-level conventions are needed to make this process work between the vast range of possible widgets, so that (for instance) cutting from a music editor and pasting into a spreadsheet works as expected. Developing suitable data transfer formats is the subject of current research, for example in the National Science Foundation's EXPRES project.

3.4.2 Window Manager

A window manager is the software and user interface for controlling the location and status of windows in a window system. It can also be defined as that portion of the user interface devoted to manipulating the presentation of multiple contexts, or windows, on behalf of the user. The window manager generally allows the user to:

create, destroy, reposition, and resize windows,

adjust the depth order of windows (move to top: "expose", or move to
  bottom: "hide"),

change the state of windows (open or closed: "iconic"),

specify which window is to accept keyboard characters (the "listener" or
  "input focus" window).

The user interface to these operations normally involves wrapping an active border around the application window, which contain controls or small icons that the user can click on or drag to invoke them.

The window manager will also implement a window layout policy. Two common policies are *overlapping* and *tiling*:

An overlapping window manager will normally ask the user to size and
  position a newly created window, perhaps by dragging out a rubber-band
  rectangle. The new window will initially appear on top of the other
  windows, but succeeding windows and user actions may cause it to be
  hidden. This concept of overlapping 2-dimensional surfaces on the screen
  is often called 2 1/2-D.

A tiling window manager, such as Star and Andrew, will normally assign a
  size and position to newly created windows automatically, and perhaps
  adjust the size or position of others, to ensure that no window overlaps
  another.

44

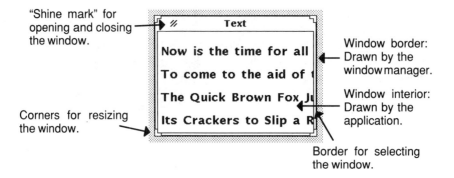

"Shine mark" for
opening and closing
the window.

Window border:
Drawn by the
window manager.

Window interior:
Drawn by the
application.

Corners for resizing
the window.

Border for selecting
the window.

Figure: 3.13. Example of an OPEN LOOK window with a border that is handled by
a window manager. The various regions in the border may be manipulated by the user, and the window manager turns these into transformations on the window.

Different layout polices are largely a matter of aesthetics, and agreement
on them has proved hard to come by. As a result, recent window systems
such as NeWS and X11 are designed to support a wide range of policies, isolating the policies in separate code that the user can easily replace[ROSE89].

3.4.3   Base Window System

The base window system has two fundamental purposes:

1   To provide the upper layers with abstractions of the physical
     resources. For example, a window is an abstraction of the physical
     screen resource.

2   To assign real physical resources to these abstract objects. For exam-
     ple, the window system will assign real pixels to the visible part of
     an abstract window.

These tasks are analogous to those of an operating system. An operating
system provides its clients (applications) with abstractions of real resources
such as CPU and memory. A window system can be thought of as an operating system that provides the user interface with multiprocessing, by
providing multiple windows on-screen to communicate with multiple applications, and virtual memory, through multiple overlapping windows that
can provide more "virtual pixels" than physical pixels.

The resources which the base window system must manage include:

the pixels on the screen(s), and any additional memory used to hold
    obscured parts of windows.

the colormap(s) that convert pixels to colors during the video refresh
   process.

the keyboard, mouse, and other input devices.

The base window system must assign these resources to multiple clients,
protect these clients so that one client's use of the real resource does not interfere with another's, and allow clients to operate on the abstract
resources it gives them.

3.4.3.1 The Screen

The user wants multiple applications to share the screen. The goal of the
window system is to provide each application the illusion that it has sole
control over its window. To maintain this illusion, the window system provides mutual protection between windows. Ideally, applications do not
draw in the coordinate space of the screen, they draw in their own "logical"
coordinate space, which should correspond to the needs of the application,
rather than the hardware characteristics of the target screen. Less advanced
window systems make applications use pixel ("real") coordinate spaces
within their windows, which decreases application portability between different display resolutions and sizes. The base window system should allow
applications to establish their own arbitrary coordinate space. It then maps
the application's logical coordinate space into the physical device (display)
space, enforcing appropriate clipping as windows overlap.
Controlling access to the screen can be compared to the control of virtual
memory in a multitasking environment. In the case of virtual memory,
many applications are contending for a physical resource, the physical RAM
(Random Access Memory) into which the application code and data segments are loaded for execution. The sum of the memory requirements for
the simultaneous execution of all applications on the system may be much
too large for the amount of physical memory available. Therefore, a large
logical memory area is mapped into a smaller physical memory area "on
demand," or as an application takes its turn to execute.
The window system provides a roughly similar mapping algorithm. First,
the window system must provide a logical-to-physical mapping for all visible applications at all times. Second, the window system needs to have a
response to applications whose logical resources (such as a coordinate space
of 3000 by 3000) have no possible one-to-one correspondence with the physical resources available (e.g., a window partially covering a 1000 by 1000
pixel screen). The logical screen space required can be stretched (or shrunk)
to fit the physical space available. Docs and NeWS are examples of systems
with such transform capabilities. Otherwise the user or the application has
to pan the window to cover the one-to-one logical to physical mapping.

46

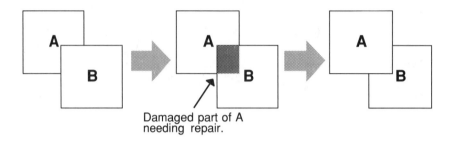

Damaged part of A
needing repair.

Figure: 3.14.   Partially visible window, A, being uncovered. The shaded area shows
the portion of the window which was damaged as a result.

Managing the screen area also includes managing *damage* repair. Applications may draw into windows which are completely or partly hidden by other windows. If the obscuring window is removed, the pixels in the newly revealed area must be changed from showing the image of the old window to showing the image of the new window. The pixels are said to be *damaged*. The process of re-painting them to show the new image is called *damage repair*.

The window system can use various strategies for damage repair:

It can maintain off-screen memory containing the obscured pixels, and copy the damaged area to the screen from this buffer. This technique is called "backing store" or "retained windows".

It can maintain a display list, or other representation of the operations needed to paint a window, and re-execute these operations when required to paint the damaged area.

It can signal the appropriate client that damage has occurred and depend on it to repaint the damaged area.

Each strategy has advantages and disadvantages:

Retaining windows is effective, simple and fast, but can consume large amounts of memory. Retaining a 1024 by 1024 image in 8 bits deep color requires a megabyte of memory. And retaining an off-screen image only *reduces* damage. It cannot eliminate damage caused, for example, by windows being resized.

Display lists are often a more compact encoding of the re-created image, but may be slower. And some applications may not be able to represent their damage repair as a display list.

Depending on the client to repair the damage can cause problems for
applications, such as image-processing, which operate directly on the
pixels without maintaining an internal representation of the image.

Since none of the strategies is wholly satisfactory, window systems generally use a mix of them and allow each window to select the strategy that
works best for them. NeWS supports all three strategies. Windows can
optionally be retained, applications can down-load a program that knows
how to repair damage into the server (emulating a display list), or the application can decide to repair the damage itself. If the client decides to repair
the damage itself, it can find out the exact shape of the damaged area, and
repaint only that part of the image to save time. In general, retaining windows is the fastest but most expensive method, and direct client repair is
the simplest. Clients using retained windows will have to implement direct
repair as well, as a fall-back for cases such as resizing where retaining fails
to eliminate damage.

3.4.3.2   The Colormap

There are additional components of typical graphics devices that the base
window system is responsible for managing. For example, many color displays have *colormaps* that convert the values stored in pixels into colors on
the screen. A color map is a table of color values that is indexed by a pixel
value. A typical color map has 256 entries, indexed by pixels that are 8 bits
deep. Each map entry has red, green, and blue components that determine the
actual color displayed for the corresponding pixel value. There are a limited
number of colors that may be displayed at one time, dictated by the number
of slots in the color map. This limit creates a resource allocation problem
that has to be managed.

The base window system will provide the upper layers of the system
with the abstraction of a number of virtual colormaps, and will implement
them by either handing out ranges of pixel values to clients, or statically
determining a set of good colors and restricting applications to using them.

X11 is an example of a system providing clients total control over the
colormap resource, whereas NeWS manages the resource internally. Chapter
10 describes how this conflict is resolved in the X11/NeWS merge.

3.4.3.3   The Input Devices

The base window system is responsible for converting external events
into a canonical form. Events include up and down transitions of keys on
the keyboard or the mouse buttons, movements of the mouse, and perhaps
system-generated events such as time-outs. After being converted into
canonical form they are:

48

1   serialized into a single stream in strict time sequence,

2   formatted into a uniform event report identifying the type of event,

3   stamped with the time of occurrence,

4   labeled with the mouse position (and the state of some or all of the keys and buttons) at the time of occurrence,

5   distributed to the appropriate window.

Strict serialization is required to provide predictable behavior when the system lags behind the user. Timestamping is required to support some user interface styles, such as double-click selection, and for serialization. Determining the appropriate window can be a complex process; windows can ignore certain classes of events, and can perhaps pre-empt other events even if they do not occur within their bounds. The window receiving events is often called the *input focus*.

In most base window systems, there are actually two input foci. One controls the distribution of mouse (and normally menu) events, and the other controls the distribution of keystrokes. Typically there are two ways of managing these foci:

1   Both foci are tied together and all events are distributed to the window under the mouse. This is often called the Focus-Follows-Cursor policy.

2   Mouse events go to the window under the mouse, but keystrokes go to some window that has been designated as the current input focus. This is often called Click-to-Type, since the user usually clicks on a window to transfer focus to it.

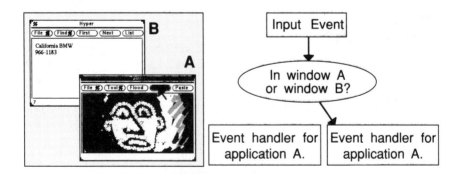

Figure: 3.15.   General input distribution: input events being generated and selectively passed to applications. One of the applications has nominated its own input handling routine by expressing interest in certain events.

The window system provides the input focus, one of these mechanisms, transparently to the toolkit. Applications are also generally unaware of the mechanism by which the input focus is specified, though they must be able to respond to the input focus being transferred to the application.

Many client applications allow the user to select objects. For example, an editor allows users to select regions of text in their documents. Window systems normally provide a mechanism help clients manage selections and to rendezvous and transfer data among themselves. They normally support several named selections, including the Primary and Secondary selections, and clients can assert ownership of a selection by name. Clients that want to retrieve the contents of a selection use the name to rendezvous with the owner of the selection and ask it to supply the data.

3.4.4   Graphics Library

The lowest level in the window system is the graphics library. It provides the upper layers with an imaging model, a set of operations that can be used to paint on the screen, and implements them in terms of the operations available from the display hardware. The operations available from the graphics library must be powerful enough to support a wide range of applications. However, implementing a powerful imaging model across a wide range of different display hardware with good performance can be hard.

The three basic features of an imaging model are:
- the coordinate system(s) it uses,
- the drawing operations it provides,
- and the font capabilities it supports.

The simplest imaging models are the ones based on the *RasterOp* (Raster Operation), also known as *bitblt* (bit block transfer) primitive. This model operates in the hardware pixel coordinate system, performing a boolean combination of the pixels in a source and a destination rectangle. Typical operations are copying a rectangle of pixels from one place to another and filling a rectangle with a color.

Early systems based on this imaging model, like the Alto, provided only lines and RasterOp as drawing operations. Text was drawn using RasterOp. Later systems, like the Macintosh, made the construction of graphically interesting interfaces easier by enhancing the imaging model. The Quick-Draw graphics library, though RasterOp based, supports curves and non-rectangular operations. As a result, QuickDraw provides the ability to construct more interesting interfaces at the cost of a somewhat more complex application programmer interface.

Imaging models capable of dealing with curves and transformations can render much more interesting images than those that just deal with straight lines in pixel coordinates. The PostScript language graphics model provides high-level graphics primitives, which give NeWS the ability to deal with

50

curves, regions that have strange shapes, images, and arbitrary transformations of them. In addition, this model operates in user-defined co-ordinates (hiding the existence of pixels) and can efficiently span a wide variety of devices.

A good example is the drawing of a rose in Figure 3.16. Without the ability to draw curves, an application would have to draw such an image using a lot of small line segments. Besides being a performance problem, it is often the case that if each individual application is left the task of supporting curves on their own, most will do a poor job.

Figure: 3.16.   PostScript 2D graphics illustrating curves and scaling.

Although PostScript provides the most advanced 2D graphics model available to date, it has no features for 3D. There are no window systems (yet) that have well integrated 3D models, although some have extensions that support some form of 3D.

portant aspect of the window system's imaging model is its
t and fonts. At a minimum, window systems provide facili-
nition of new fonts, opening and closing font libraries, and
r strings. More advanced systems provide altered spacing in
kerning, arbitrary baseline directions, and the ability to
ly large fonts. Typically, window systems define fonts
tions of bitmap images, supporting only a limited set of
ations. One of the interesting features that NeWS inherits
is the ability to dynamically scan-convert outline font rep-
bitmaps, creating characters at arbitrary sizes and rotations.

ary

portant factors influencing window system architecture are
d multiprocessing structure. Operating systems can be cate-
classes:

1   Single address space, single process.

2   Single address space, multiple processes.

3   Multiple address spaces, multiple processes.

The first class — single address space, single process — corresponds to simple operating systems, such as those on personal computers. They are simple and small, and are often just subroutine libraries. MS/DOS and the Macintosh operating system fall under this category.

The second class — single address space, multiple processes — is often found in dedicated language environments. Lisp machines, such as the Symbolics computer, and the systems from Xerox PARC are good examples. The NeWS server itself, when thought of as an "operating system," is another example of a system built under this principle.

The third class — multiple address spaces — corresponds to the operating systems derived from or developed for multi-user machines. VM, VMS, Multics, OS/2, and UNIX are all examples.

The first two classes share the advantage that every part of the system can access every piece of memory. Data structures can be shared or accessed merely by passing pointers. For instance, if an application builds a display list of graphics commands, no data copying is necessary when the window systems renders it. The window system can access the display list directly.

The last two classes, multiple processes, share the disadvantage that they have to cope with synchronization. There are shared resources that must be accessed by the multiple processes and these accesses must be arbitrated.

In a multiple-address-space environment, window systems can be partitioned by placing the bulk of their code in either the kernel, each client process, or some separate server process. All three partitioning schemes require that some information be passed between address spaces. A set of processes is trying to cooperate; this cooperation has a price, and that price is the cost of exchanging information.

Window systems that require each client to perform graphics operations by directly accessing the hardware expect high performance, but often do not achieve it due to unexpected synchronization problems. The centralized window-server architecture solves most of these problems. It incurs an added message passing cost, but the impact of this cost can be substantially reduced by careful design of the protocol.

4
Introduction to the PostScript Language

"PostScript is the future of words on paper."

Arthur C. Clarke

This chapter gives a brief introduction to the standard PostScript language, as implemented in NeWS and many thousands of PostScript printers. This introduction is not particularly rigorous, but it should offer enough information for understanding the rest of the book. For a full description, see the *PostScript Language Reference Manual*[ADOB85a].

4.1   psh

The NeWS **psh** command, entered by the user to the system command shell, provides an easy way to test the PostScript commands and programs described below. If you have NeWS available to you, use **psh** to try out the examples from the following sections: **psh** establishes a connection to the NeWS server and sends the PostScript programs you type to the server, then you can interactively program and debug the NeWS server. For the purposes of this chapter, consider **psh** a way to preview standard PostScript programs on the screen. However, **psh** is demonstrated in the chapters ahead as a means to also test and run complex NeWS programs.

There are some differences between interacting with NeWS using the **psh** command and interacting with a PostScript printer. First, some printer-related commands, such as **showpage**, operate differently in the NeWS environment. Second, the coordinate systems of a standard PostScript printer and a NeWS window may differ. The default LaserWriter coordinate scheme goes from (0,0) to (612,792), whereas a NeWS canvas can be any size.

Usually, you connect to the NeWS server using the **psh** command, then you type the **executive** operator to start an *executive*, an interactive session with the server. Commands are typed in as follows:

```
system prompt% psh
executive
Welcome to NeWS Version 1.1
```

Once running an executive, you can type in arbitrary PostScript commands.

4.2   Conventions

All the PostScript commands in this and following chapters can be tested by typing them into the **psh** executive. In the **psh** examples, bold text indicates indicates system response. Regular text indicates commands typed in by the user. Unquoted bold text within the descriptive text denote NeWS or PostScript operators. Newly defined words, variables and values are italicized. These conventions are followed throughout the remainder of the book.

4.3   Syntax

A PostScript program is a stream of characters. This stream of characters is broken up by the PostScript interpreter into a sequence of *tokens*. A token is usually delimited by spaces, but a few special characters also delimit tokens (like braces and the percent sign). Tokens represent *objects*. So:

```
100 150 moveto (Hello world!) show
```

is made up of five tokens: the two numbers *100* and *150*, the keyword **moveto**, the string *Hello world!* and the keyword **show**. These tokens are translated into integer, keyword and string *objects*. Objects are manipulated internally by the PostScript language.

4.3.1   Numbers

Number tokens are just sequences of digits with an optional decimal point and "E" format exponent, like you would see in Fortran or C. Some valid numbers are *100*, *100.75*, *1.0075E2* and *1000E-1*. Number tokens are translated into number objects that are either of type *integer* or *real*.

4.3.2 Strings

String tokens in PostScript are sequences of characters surrounded by parenthesis: "(" and ")". These character sequences are translated into objects of type *string*. They follow the C language convention for special characters, so that, for example:

```
(Hello!\n)
```

is a string that contains 7 characters, the last of which is a newline, indicated by "\n".

4.3.3 Comments

Everything from a "%" up until the end of the line is a comment. Comments are completely ignored:

```
% this will be ignored
```

4.3.4 Keywords

Keywords tokens are sequences of characters that do not look like numbers, strings or comments. *K*, *add*, *sum*, *this-thing*, and *j10* are all keywords. Keywords serve the purpose of identifiers in other languages. Like Lisp atoms, they are real objects, not just compile-time symbols that represent something else. A very important property of keyword objects is that if two *look* the same, then they *are* the same — they are equal.

All objects have a flag that indicates whether or not they are *executable*. The meaning of this will be explained later. Normally, on numbers and strings the executable flag is off. For keywords, the flag is normally on. A slash character ("/") written in front of a keyword indicates that it should not be executable. Thus, *sum* and */sum* are the same keyword, except that the first is executable, and the second is not.

4.3.5 Arrays

Array objects are linear collections of other objects, distinguished by enclosing the array objects in either square brackets "[ ]", or brace brackets "{ }". Arrays written with square brackets are not executable, and arrays written with brace brackets are executable. As an example:

```
[ heinz 57 (tasty!) ]
```

is a non-executable array that contains three objects: the executable keyword *heinz*, the number *57* and the string *tasty!*. Similarly,

```
{ heinz 57 (tasty!) }
```

is the same array, now executable. There is a "catch" in the syntax of non-executable arrays that will be explained later.

4.3.6 Other Data Types

There are many other PostScript data types. The following list presents the most important. Others will be mentioned in the pages that follow:

boolean   The two special values **true** and **false**.

dictionary   A table that associates *values* with *keys*. Keys in dictionaries do not have to be keywords — they can be any PostScript language object. See section 4.5.4 for more information about dictionaries.

marker   Objects which mark the stack to delimit groups of objects on the stack.

null   A unique value used to represent the null value or "nothing".

operator   Operator objects refer to operations that PostScript can perform. For example, there is an operator to add two numbers and one to draw a string.

4.4 Stacks

The PostScript language makes extensive use of several *stacks*. Stacks represent locations where objects are temporarily stored. Everything in the PostScript language operates on these stacks, even variable definitions and control statements. Operators take their operands from the stack, and push the objects returned onto the stack. The language actually has four separate stacks that store data (*operand stack*), commands (*execution stack*), local storage context or lists of dictionary objects (*dictionary stack*), and graphic settings (*graphic state stack*). The stack colloquially referred to as *the stack* is the operand stack.

4.5   Execution

Now that we have some background, we can talk about what PostScript programs are and how they execute. A PostScript program is just a sequence of PostScript objects. The expression 2 3 add is parsed into a sequence of three tokens, which in turn become three PostScript objects: the integer *2*, the integer *3*, and the keyword **add**. A sequence is executed by taking each object in turn and executing the object individually. The execution of an object depends on its type, according to the following rules:

An executable operator executes the action denoted by that operator.

An executable keyword is looked up in the dictionary stack. The dictionary stack is a set of dictionaries that provide the naming context for a PostScript program. After the keyword is looked up, the object found is executed. A special case is made for executable arrays. The array is pushed on the execution stack and is executed as a sequence of objects.

If the type of the object is neither a keyword nor an executable operator, then the object is pushed on to the operand stack.

Let's look more closely at the execution of **"2 3 add"**. When the first object, the number *2*, is encountered, it is pushed onto the operand stack since it is neither an executable operator nor an executable keyword. Processing of *3* is identical. *add* is an executable keyword, so the second rule applies: *add* is looked up in the dictionary stack. The dictionary at the top of the stack is searched to determine if any value exists under the key **add**. If no key exists, then the next dictionary down in the stack is examined, until a key is found or the entire dictionary stack is examined. For this example, we assume that a value is eventually found, and that it is an executable operator. The PostScript interpreter executes this object, causing some action to occur. In this case, the **add** operator (as opposed to the **add** keyword) is the value found, and it pops the top two entries from the operand stack and pushes their sum onto the operand stack.

Procedures in PostScript are simply executable arrays. When a keyword is looked up in the process of executing a sequence of objects, and the value of the keyword is an executable array, then that executable array gets executed as a sequence of objects. It is important to remember that if an executable array occurs in a sequence, it is not executed: it is only pushed on the operand stack. It will only be executed if it is found as the value of a keyword or if some operator explicitly executes it (more on this later).

The bottom element of the dictionary stack is normally a dictionary known as *systemdict*. This dictionary contains all the operators defined by the PostScript language. The second from the bottom is a dictionary known as *userdict* that contains user defined local variables.

4.6 The PostScript Language Operators

The PostScript language is commonly perceived as a graphics language, but in fact it has a full set of general-purpose operators. These operators are used for such varied purposes as arithmetic, manipulating data structures, control flow, and, of course, for graphics.

4.6.1 Arithmetic

When an operator is defined it is presented in the following format:

i_1 i_2...i_n **name** o_1 o_2...o_n

> The operator **name** pops its input parameters $i_1, i_2,...i_n$ from the stack, performs some computation based on them and pushes its output parameters $o_1, o_2,...o_n$ onto the stack when it is done. If the operator takes no inputs or returns no results, then an em dash (—) will appear in the description.

Arithmetic operators exist for all the commonly used arithmetic functions. There are the binary operators **add**, **sub**, **mul**, **div**, **idiv**, **and**, **or**, **xor** and **mod**. Unary operators include **abs**, **round**, **floor**, **ceiling**, **truncate**, **neg** and **not**, and the relationals **lt**, **le**, **gt**, **ge**, **ne** and **eq**.

a b **add** c
Pops a and b from the stack and pushes c, their sum, on to the stack.

a b **sub** c
$c = a - b$

a b **mul** c
$c = a * b$

a b **div** c
$c = a / b$ (real division).

a b **idiv** c
$c = a / b$ (integer division).

a b **and** c
$c = a \mathbin{\&} b$ (bitwise **and** and boolean **and**).

a b **or** c
$c = a \mid b$ (bitwise **or** and boolean **or**).

a b **xor** c
$c = a \wedge b$ (bitwise **exclusive or** and boolean **exclusive or**).

a b **mod** c
$c = a \mathbin{\%} b$ (remainder after integer division).

a **abs** b
$b = |a|$ (absolute value).

a **round** b
$b = a$ rounded to the nearest integer.

a **floor** b
$b =$ the largest integer less than or equal to a.

a **ceiling** b $\quad$ b = the smallest integer greater that or equal to *a*.

a **truncate** b

$\qquad$ b = *a* with its fractional part removed (**truncate** is equivalent to **floor** if *a* is positive, and to **ceiling** otherwise).

a **neg** b $\qquad$ b = -*a*

a **not** b $\qquad$ b = ~*a* (boolean not).

a b **lt** c $\qquad$ c = **true** if *a*<*b*, **false** otherwise.

a b **le** c $\qquad$ c = **true** if *a*≤*b*, **false** otherwise.

a b **gt** c $\qquad$ c = **true** if *a*>*b*, **false** otherwise.

a b **ge** c $\qquad$ c = **true** if *a*≥*b*, **false** otherwise.

a b **ne** c $\qquad$ c = **true** if *a*≠*b*, **false** otherwise.

a b **eq** c $\qquad$ c = **true** if *a*=*b*, **false** otherwise.

Let's look at the execution of "**14 27 add 2 div round**":

Operator	Stack	Comment
14	14	push the integer *14* onto the stack.
27	14 27	push the integer *27* onto the stack.
add	41	Looks up the keyword **add**. **add** will be found in systemdict to be the operator that replaces the top two elements of the stack with their sum.
2	41 2	push the integer *2* onto the stack.
div	20.5	Divides *41* by *2*.
round	21	Rounds *20.5* to the nearest integer.

4.6.2 Stack Manipulation

Some operators exist for the purpose of manipulating the stack only:

a **pop** — $\quad$ Removes the top element from the stack.

a **dup** a a $\quad$ Duplicates the top of the stack.

$i_n...i_0$ n **index** $i_n...i_0\ i_n$

$\qquad$ Duplicates the *nth* element from the top of the stack (*0* **index** is the same as **dup**).

$i_n...i_0$ n **icopy** $i_n...i_0$ $i_n...i_{0n}$
> Duplicates the n elements on the top of the stack (1 **copy** is the same as **dup**).

a b **exch** b a Exchanges the top two elements of the stack.

$i_1...i_m$ m n **roll** $i_{m-n+1}..i_m$ $i_1..i_{m-n}$
> Rotates the top m elements n places (*2 1* **roll** is the same as **exch**.).

Let's look at the execution of ``(is) (now) exch 1 index 3 2 roll'':

Operator	Stack	Comment
(is)	(is)	Push the string *is* onto the stack.
(now)	(is) (now)	
		Push the string *now* onto the stack.
exch	(now) (is)	
		Exchange the top two elements
1	(now) (is) 1	
		Push the integer *1* onto the stack
index	(now) (is) (now)	
		Duplicates the string *now* to the top of the stack.
3 2 roll	(is) (now) (now)	
		Rotate the top three elements of the stack.

4.6.3   Dictionaries

A dictionary is a table that contains pairs of *key-value* objects. Dictionaries are the ubiquitous way of storing and accessing information within the PostScript language interpreter. Dictionaries act as databases for system and program information. They are structured as groups of key-value pairs. A key is usually a keyword object (such as */sum*), although it may be any kind of object, while a value may be any object. The PostScript language defines a set of operators to manipulate the contents of dictionaries:

n **dict** dict   Creates a dictionary with enough room for n pairs. Initially, none will be in use.

dict object **get** value
> Looks into the dictionary for the pair whose key is *object* and returns the corresponding value.

dict key value **put** —

>Stores the pair *key value* in *dict*. If a pair with a matching *key* already exists in the dictionary, it will be replaced.

The PostScript language interpreter maintains a dictionary stack that stores the set of dictionaries in use. The order of the dictionaries on the stack determines the order in which the dictionaries will be accessed. With this mechanism PostScript programs can maintain a local set of data or program definitions. The last dictionary pushed onto the stack is accessed first, other dictionaries are accessed in their order on the stack if the reference is not found. Therefore, if a user program redefines a key that already exists, the new definition will be found in the topmost dictionary, stopping the key search. The top dictionary on the stack is called the *current dictionary*, and all keys referenced in a program are first searched for in the current dictionary.

There are two standard dictionaries that are always present on the stack — *systemdict* and *userdict*. All of the system operators are stored in systemdict. Whenever a new PostScript user program begins, it is given a new userdict dictionary where the bulk of user key-values are defined.

Here are some operators for dictionaries and the dictionary stack:

— **currentdict** dict

>Returns the current dictionary: the dictionary on the top of the dictionary stack.

dict **begin** —

>Pushes *dict* onto the dictionary stack. *dict* becomes the current dictionary.

— **end** —   Pops a dictionary from the top of the dictionary stack.

key value **def** —

>Stores the pair *key value* in the current dictionary. It is exactly equivalent to "**currentdict key value put**". **def** is the operator that is normally used to define variables.

key **load** value

>Scans the dictionary stack for a dictionary that contains *key* and pushes that value onto the operand stack. *load* is very similar to normal variable access (keyword lookup in the process of executing a sequence) except that it always pushes the value on to the operand stack: *load* never tries to evaluate it.

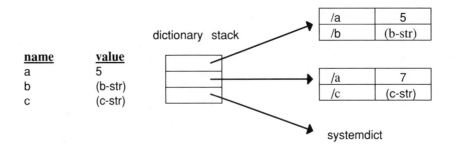

/a	5
/b	(b-str)

/a	7
/c	(c-str)

dictionary stack

name	value
a	5
b	(b-str)
c	(c-str)

systemdict

Figure: 4.1.   The name search for a newly defined variable — stack with system-dict, userdict, and currentdict on the stack and an instance of the redefinition of a key that is in two places.

Let's look at another example "`/sum 2 2 add def`":

Operator	Stack	Comment
/sum	/sum	push keyword, since /sum is non-executable.
2	/sum 2	push integer 2.
2	/sum 2 2	push integer 2.
add	/sum 4	Since add is executable, it gets looked up in the dictionary stack, is found in systemdict, and its operator object gets executed to add the two values.
def	empty	Stores the value 4 into the dictionary on the top of the stack (currentdict) under the key sum.

Without explaining all operator references, the following is an example of dictionary use. Unlike previous examples, it is presented as a typescript of a **psh** session:

`% psh`	Invoke psh as a UNIX shell command.
`executive`	Tell NeWS that we're an interactive session, not a program. Otherwise if we make any mistakes NeWS will break the connection.

`Welcome to NeWS Version 1.1`

`/mydict 10 dict def`

                    Create a dictionary, name it *mydict*.

`mydict ==`   Print it out.

dict[ ]   It is empty.

`mydict /var 23 put`

                    Associate the value *23* with the key *var*.

`mydict ==`   Once again print the dictionary.

dict[/var:23]

                    Note that *var* is now defined in *mydict*.

`mydict 23 /var put`

                    This time, use *23* as the key rather than the value.

`mydict ==`   Look at the value again.

dict[23:/var

    /var:23] Note the two entries.

`mydict /var get ==`

                    Get the value of *var* from the dictionary.

23   It is what was expected.

`mydict begin`

                    Push *mydict* onto the dictionary stack.

`var`   Now normal variable lookups will look there.

`==`

23   The "variable" *var* comes from *mydict*.

`/var 77 def`   Change the value of *var*.

`/var2 23 def`

                    Define a new keyword/value.

`mydict ==`   Look at *mydict*.

dict[23:/var

    /var2:23 This is where *var2* got defined.

    /var:77] The value of *var* changed.

`end`   Pop *mydict* from the dictionary stack.

`var`   Access *var* as a simple variable.

ERROR

Process: 0x3C783C Error: undefined

64

Stack: dictionary[22]

> *var* is undefined because the dictionary in which it is
> defined is no longer anywhere on the dictionary stack.

Executing: var

At: Reading file(?,W,R)

★★★★★

A dictionary is a composite object; it is made up of other objects. Other
composite objects include arrays and strings. Composite objects behave differently from simple objects in some cases. One of the most significant is
copying an object. When a composite object is copied, its data is not dupli-
cated. Only a pointer (or a reference) to the object is passed to the requestor
of the copy, which conserves memory and also allows data sharing to take
place easily among cooperating PostScript programs. This attribute encourages the object-oriented structure of the NeWS Lite toolkit, discussed in
Chapter 6.

4.6.4 Arrays

An array object is simply a list of other objects. This array is indexed by
integers starting at 0. Here are some common array operators:

n **array** array
> Creates an array of length *n* on the stack. All entries will
> be null.

array n **get** value
> Gets the *n*th element from *array*.

array n value **put** —
> Puts *value* into the *n*th element of *array*.

array **length** len
> Returns the number of elements in *array*.

The following simple example shows an interactive session using arrays:

`% psh`   Connect to the NeWS server.

`executive`   Tell it we want an interactive session.

Welcome to NeWS Version 1.1

`/arr 3 array def`
> Create a *3* element array and assign it to a variable.

`arr ==`   Print out the array.

[null null null]

> It starts out filled with *null*'s.

```
arr 0 (Hello) put
```

> Put the string *Hello* into the zeroth element.

```
arr ==
```

[(Hello) null null]

> Now it contains the string and the nulls.

```
arr 1 4 put
```

> Fill in the other elements: *4* in second element (the first element has index 0, the second has index 1, ...).

```
arr 2 /key put
```

> Place */key* in third element. Note the different types.

```
arr ==
```

[(Hello) 4 /key]

```
arr 2 get ==
```

> Fetch value at *2*nd array element from the array.

/key   The value is what we put there.

The catch in the syntax of non-executable arrays: "[" and "]" are actually operators. "[" pushes a mark on the stack, and "]" takes everything on the stack above the mark and makes an array out of them. The mark is removed from the stack and the array is pushed on. The PostScript code between "[" and "]" is therefore executed *before* the array is built. In contrast, "{" and "}" are handled by the parser. Here is an example:

```
% psh
executive
```

Welcome to NeWS Version 1.1

```
{ 2 2 add } ==
```

> Type in an executable array.

{2 2 add}   Notice that when we print it, the array contains the objects that we typed in.

```
[2 2 add] ==
```

> Type almost the same thing, but using [ ] instead.

[4]   Notice that **2 2 add** was evaluated.

4.6.5   Control flow Operators

The PostScript language has many operators that control the flow of execution. There is nothing that resembles a *goto*. Control flow is handled by a mechanism that looks like procedure calls: the operators take executable arrays (referred to as *proc* parameters) and execute their contents. Here are some of them:

boolean proc **if** —

>If *boolean* is true, *proc*, an executable array, will get executed.

boolean proc$_1$ proc$_2$ **ifelse** —

>If *boolean* is true, *proc$_1$* will get executed, otherwise *proc$_2$*.

>proc **loop** —
>Executes *proc* forever —or until something in *proc* executes the *exit*.

— **exit** —   Exits the innermost loop. It can be used to exit any kind of loop.

n proc **repeat** —

>Similar to *loop* except that it only executes *proc n* times.

lo inc hi proc **for** —

>Pushes *lo* onto the stack, compares *hi* to the current top of the stack. If they are not equal, it executes *proc* and increments the value on the top of the stack by *inc*. If *inc* is negative, then the loop proceeds in the reverse order.

obj proc **forall** —

>Executes *proc* for each element of *obj*.

4.7   A Small Example

So far we have presented some of the important non-graphic operators of the PostScript language. The following PostScript function illustrates them in action:

```
/min {
    2 dict begin
```
> Create a dictionary for local storage and push it onto the dictionary stack.

```
    /a exch def
```
> Save the top of the stack in *a*.

```
    /b exch def
```
> And the next in *b*.

```
    a b lt
```
> Compare *a* and *b*.

```
      { a }
```
> Code fragment to push *a* onto the stack.

```
      { b }
```
> Code fragment to push *b* onto the stack.

```
    ifelse
```
> Execute the first code fragment if *a* is less than *b*, the second otherwise.

```
    end
```
Remove the local variable dictionary from the stack.

```
} def
```
Define *min* to be the preceding executable array. Remember: executable arrays are procedures.

```
4 7 min
```
Invoke our newly defined function.

```
==
```
Print out the result.

4

This PostScript program defines a function called *min* by defining the keyword *min* to have a code fragment as its value. The code fragment begins by creating a dictionary and pushing it onto the dictionary stack **(2 dict begin)**. This creates a place for local variables. Next *a* and *b* are assigned the values of the parameters to *min* which were passed to it on the stack. The variables *a* and *b* are then compared **(a b lt)** and either **{ a }** or **{ b }** is executed to push the lesser of the two onto the stack. Finally **end** is used to remove the local variables from the dictionary stack.

While the use of dictionaries for local variables is reasonably clear and understandable, it is usually preferable to avoid them when possible and just keep temporaries on the stack. Here is a significantly more efficient version of the *min* function:

68

```
/min {
        2 copy gt
```
        Compare *a* and *b*.

```
        { exch } if
```
        if *a* is greater than *b*, exchange them, leaving the largest on the top of the stack.

```
        pop
```
        Pop the largest from the stack.

```
} def
```

4.8   The Stencil/Paint Imaging Model: Paths

The PostScript language implements the stencil/paint imaging model, incorporating the concept of a *path*. A path is an arbitrary sequence of points, straight lines, and curves that describe some shape. This shape may be closed and enclose a region, or it may be a line trajectory. Many operators can be used to modify a path. Once a path is built, it can be filled with paint, drawn as a line, or treated as a clipping boundary for further graphic operators. Like the current dictionary, the PostScript language maintains the concept of a *current path*, which is the path currently being constructed and manipulated. The current path can be explicitly or implicitly defined by the user program. Some operators such as **stroke**, **fill**, and **clip** automatically construct a new current path upon their completion. Otherwise, a new current path can be started by using the **newpath** command. Unlike many other graphics languages, every operator that needs a geometric description of an outline as an argument gets it in exactly the same way — from the current path. This principle guarantees consistency between the operators.

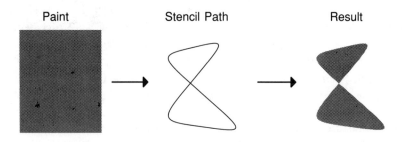

Figure: 4.2.   Paths and paint.

One way to think of a path is as a silkscreen or a stencil. When drawing an object, first construct a path (stencil) and apply color (ink) through it. Figure 4.1 shows a large patch of color that is pressed through a path. Images can be used as inks as well as uniform colors.

When a path is constructed, it is built from pieces by operators such as **lineto**. **lineto** takes two parameters, the x and y coordinates of the endpoint of the line. The line starts at the *current point*, defined with the **moveto** command. After **lineto** has been executed, the endpoint becomes the start point of the next line. By contrast, **moveto** sets the current point, but does not add a line segment to the path. Here are a few of the path construction operators:

— **newpath** —

> Empties the current path.

x y **moveto** —

> Set the current point to x,y.

x y **lineto** —

> Add a straight line segment from the current point to x,y.

x y r as ae **arc** —

> Add an arc to the path whose center is at *x,y* and has radius *r*. The arc starts at angle *as* and continues counterclockwise until angle *ae*. Before adding the arc, a straight line segment is added to the path that goes from the current point to the beginning of the arc. After adding the arc, the current point will be at the end of the arc.

x1 y1 x2 y2 x3 y3 **curveto** —

> Adds a cubic *bezier* to the path which starts at the current point and ends at *x3,y3* whose two control points are *x1,y1* and *x2, y2*.

— **closepath** —

> Adds a straight line segment from the current point to the beginning of the current segment — the point that was last moved to with **moveto**.

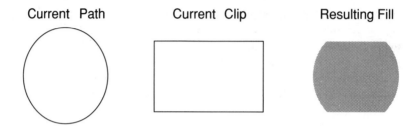

Current Path   Current Clip   Resulting Fill

Figure: 4.3.   Clipping.

Once a path is established, there are few simple things that can be done with it:

— **fill** —   Fills the current path with the current color (see Section 4.11 for more discussion of color).

— **clip** —   Intersects the *current clip path* with the current path. Whenever a graphics operation is performed, it is constrained to operate only within the current clip path. For example, whenever you fill a path, that path will be intersected with the current clip path to get the region to fill.

4.9   Transformation Matrices

The coordinates passed to these path construction operators are always transformed using the *current transformation matrix* (CTM). The CTM maps coordinates specified by a PostScript program into device coordinates. This transformation can be used to scale, rotate, skew, and translate a path. This transformation is always present; it is a fundamental concept of the PostScript language imaging model. Although the transformation can never be avoided, its overhead can be negligible, as in the case of the identity transformation, where the coordinates specified by the PostScript program map directly into device coordinates and no actual transformation is performed. In the NeWS PostScript interpreter, nine different special forms of the transformation matrices are recognized and optimized.

There are a number of operators that manipulate the CTM:

x y **translate** —
                Move the origin of the coordinate system to *x,y*.

a **rotate** —   Rotate the coordinate system of the image by *a* degrees.

xf yf **scale** —
                Scale the coordinate system by *xf* in the *x* direction and *yf* in the *y* direction.

Below is the code fragment that drew the rotated "Text" from figure 4.4:

```
10 10 scale  Expand the coordinate system.
5 1 translate
             Move the origin.
40 rotate    Rotate about the origin.
1 1 moveto   Move to 1,1 in the new coordinate system.
(Text) show  Draw the string.
```

4.10 Color

The color model in the PostScript language is simple. Color is the paint in the paint/stencil model. There is a *current color* that is used whenever anything is filled or stroked. It can be defined in one of three ways:

n setgray —

Sets the current color to be a grey value determined by *n* which ranges from 0, for black, to 1 for white.

r g b setrgbcolor —

Sets the current color to be a combination of read, green and blue as measured by r, *g* and *b* (which range from 0 to 1).

h s b sethsbcolor —

Sets the current color to a specific hue, saturation and brightness.

Figure: 4.4.   Text being rendered in a translated, scaled and rotated coordinate system. The CTM is applied to everything.

4.11   Imaging

The PostScript language supplies general facilities for displaying raster images. Images are described in a way that is completely independent of the kind of output device upon which the image will be displayed. They can be scaled, rotated, and skewed so that they can be placed in an arbitrary parallelogram on the page. The image operators base their actions on three pieces of information:

The image. This consists of a specification of the width and height in pixels of the image, the depth in bits of each pixel, and the pixels themselves.

The destination for the image: the parallelogram into which the image is to be rendered. This is implicitly specified by the current transformation matrix: the image is rendered into the rectangle with the lower left corner at user coordinate 0,0, and the upper right at 1,1. This *unit rectangle* can be placed anywhere on the page by manipulating the current transformation matrix.

A specification of how the pixels are to be rendered. This consists of both a mapping from grey values in the image to grey values in the result, and the layout of a halftone screen.

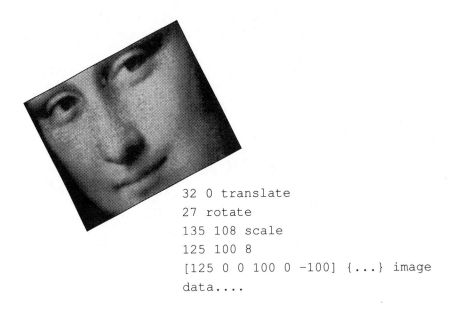

```
32 0 translate
27 rotate
135 108 scale
125 100 8
[125 0 0 100 0 -100] {...} image
data....
```

Figure: 4.5.   Figure 4.5 shows an image being rendered in a rotated and scaled coordinate system.

w h d matrix proc **image** —

> Renders an image measured *w×h×d*. *proc* is a procedure that
> is repeatedly called by **image** to return the data for the pixels
> of the image as a string. It need not return all of the pixels
> at once: **image** will call it again if it needs more. The *matrix*
> argument specifies a mapping from the unit square to the
> pixels in the image: the first pixel is at coordinate 0,0 at the
> lower left corner, the last pixel is w,h at the upper right
> corner. A common use for the *matrix* argument is to flip the
> image so that the top line, rather than the bottom line, comes
> first in the data.

w h invert matrix proc **imagemask** —

> This is similar to **image** except that the image is a 1 bit deep
> mask that defines where paint (the current color) is to be
> applied. If *invert* is true, 1 pixels are painted in the current
> color, 0 pixels are not disturbed. Otherwise 0's are painted,
> and 1's are not.

The program fragment begins by translating the origin, then scaling it up
by a factor of *100* in *x* and *y*, and then rotating it *27* degrees. An image is
then displayed inside the rectangle in the new coordinate system *0,0* to *1,1*.

4.12   Composite Operations: Lines

Almost everything else in the PostScript language graphics model is
based on these three concepts: *paths*, *transforms*, and *colors*. Even line drawing is expressed through these concepts. The **stroke** primitive is used for
drawing lines. It draws a line based on the current path according to the current line style.

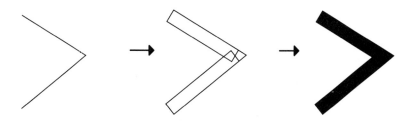

Figure: 4.6.   Stroking a path.

74

However, **stroke** is not conceptually a primitive; it is actually a combination of the **strokepath** and **fill** primitives. **fill** fills the region bounded by a closed path; **fill** is used to press ink through a stencil. **strokepath** is an operator (that can be written entirely in a PostScript program) that iterates over the current path and replaces it with a path that encloses the current path. For example, straight line segments are replaced by rectangles that enclose the segment and are of the correct width.

4.13   Composite Operations: Text

Text is similarly based on paths and ink. When drawing a letter like "L" a path is generated that bounds the character, and that path is then filled. Text is based on paths, and paths are subject to transformations, which is why text is always transformed in a way that can be predicted by looking at the CTM.

The text model is not quite as simple as the illustration indicates. Each character is actually represented by a procedure that is invoked when the character needs to be drawn. The procedure will usually generate a path and fill it, but it can also generate a path and stroke it, or use a bitmap image.

Since the text model sounds so general, it initially appears expensive, too. In reality, there are many implementation tricks that increase efficiency in all implementations of PostScript language interpreters. For example, the text model allows a cache to be used that saves the execution results of the character drawing procedures as bitmaps. When a character needs to be rendered, this cache is checked first. If an earlier procedure call was made to render that character, the cached results are used directly, without having to again call the procedure defining that character. Similarly, when lines are being drawn, if the transformed line width is less than or equal to the size of a pixel, then specialized high-speed algorithms are used.

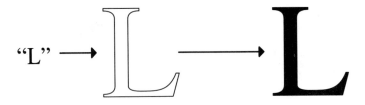

Figure: 4.7.   Painting a character.

The appearance of a character is defined by its font. Fonts are a special collection of routines to draw the characters and symbols of a typeface such as Times-Roman, Helvetica, Courier, Gothic, and Kanji. A font in the Post-Script language is a dictionary. Like any other dictionary, the font dictionary contains fields that describe the properties of the font: how to render it, metrics, encoding information (e.g., ASCII or EBCDIC), its name and other characteristics. Fonts are an extremely important, and complex, part of the PostScript language model; the details are in the *PostScript Language Reference Manual*[ADOB85a].

The **show** operator is used to draw a string of characters. It takes the string to be drawn as its only parameter. The string is drawn starting at the current position using the *current font* and the CTM.

The current position, established by **moveto**, is advanced by **show**. The *current font* is set by **setfont**, whose parameter is a font dictionary. Font dictionaries may be obtained, given the font name, by **findfont**.

These are the font manipulation operators:

font setfont —
> Sets the current font to *font*.

name findfont font
> Looks up the named font object in a global dictionary called FontDirectory: all defined fonts can be found there.
> FontDirectory contains fonts whose height is 1.

font n scalefont font
> Scales *font* by *n*.

key dict definefont font
> Defines a new *font* in FontDirectory under the given *key* that is described by the dictionary.

Using the above operators, a simple Times-Roman, 12-point character string would be drawn as follows:

```
/Times-Roman findfont
```
> Locate the font we want to use.

```
12 scalefont
```
> Scale it to be 12 points high.

```
setfont
```
Make it be the current font.

```
100 100 moveto
```
> Set the current point.

```
(Hello world!) show
```
             Draw the string.

4.14   Graphics State Components

The various objects that are described by the graphics model are contained inside an object called the *graphics state*. The *current graphics state* contains the objects that are used by the graphics operators. So far we've seen a few of the components of the graphics state:

The current path.

The current transformation matrix.

The current color.

Two primitives manipulate the entire graphics state as an object. **gsave** saves a copy of the current graphics context on a special stack, and **grestore** restores the graphics state from this stack. **gsave** and **grestore** are used when you wish to (1) *preserve* the graphics state, (2) *alter* the current graphics state in a way that is destructive, and then (3) *restore* the changed graphics state. For example, suppose that you wanted to draw a circle that was both filled with 50% gray and edged in black. Since the **fill** and **stroke** operators leave the current path empty when they are done, you would have to construct the circle twice. Creating the circle twice can be avoided by saving the state (including the path) before filling the circle, and restoring the state before edging the circle, as shown in the following example:

```
newpath
```
             Make sure that the path is cleared.

```
400 400 200 0 360 arc
```
             Construct the circular path.

```
gsave
```
             Save the state (including the current path).

```
.5 setgray fill
```
             Fill the circle with 50% gray.

```
grestore
```
             Restore the state (especially the current path).

```
0 setgray stroke
```
             Edge the circle in black.

Other important components of the graphics state are the following:

clip   This is a second path, different from the "current" path. All graphics operations are clipped against it. Note that since the *clip* is a general path, you can clip to any shape at all.

dash pattern An array describing how a line is to be dashed.

flatness   The accuracy of curves. This measures the maximum distance that the rendered curve is allowed to deviate from the true curve. More accurate curves (smaller values of flatness) are generally slower to draw.

font   The font used for text rendering.

halftone screen

        Describes the shape, angle and frequency of the halftone screen used to render greyscale values on black and white devices.

line cap   Describes the shape of the cap at the ends of a stroked line (0=>square butt ends, 1=>round ends, 2=>square ends that project).

line join   Describes the shape of the joint between line segments (0=>mitered, 1=>rounded, 2=>beveled).

line width The width of lines when they are stroked measured relative to the CTM.

miter limit How long a miter can be before it is converted to a bevel (when you have an acute angle, a mitered corner generates a sharp projection that can get very long, in these cases the joint can be converted to a bevel).

position   The current position is a coordinate in user space. It is generally the last coordinate referenced by a path construction operator.

transfer   A function that maps user gray levels into device gray levels.

Along with these graphics state components, there is a set of operators to manipulate them:

```
n setlinecap / currentlinecap

n setlinejoin / currentlinejoin

n setlinewidth / currentlinewidth

n setmiterlimit / currentmiterlimit
```

78

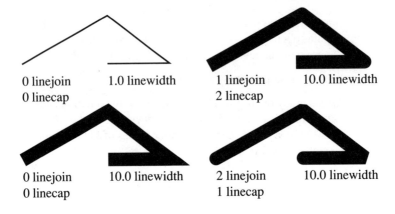

| 0 linejoin
0 linecap | 1.0 linewidth | 1 linejoin
2 linecap | 10.0 linewidth |
| 0 linejoin
0 linecap | 10.0 linewidth | 2 linejoin
1 linecap | 10.0 linewidth |

Figure: 4.8.   A line rendered several times with different values of the various parameters.

The line style parameters (dash, width, join, cap, and miter limit) are a little hard to understand without an example. Figure 4.8 shows a line rendered several times with different values of the various parameters.

4.15   A PostScript program

The following example program fills its clip path with a fan of lines. It will be used in chapter 7 as the paint method for a window:

```
/fanoflines {
```
This draws a fan of lines from 0,0 to the top and left edges. The number of lines in the fan is passed on the top of the stack.

```
gsave
```
Preserve the graphics state.

```
0 setgray
```
Set the current color to black.

```
matrix currentmatrix
```
Push a copy of the *current matrix* onto the stack.

```
exch
```
Exchange it with the number of lines parameter to get the number of lines onto the top of the stack.

```
clippath pathbbox
```

Find the bounding box of the current *clip path*, which will be the *bounding box* of the window. This leaves the x and y of the lower left hand corner on the stack followed by the width and height of the window.

scale   Scale the coordinate system by the width and height. This yields a coordinate system that ranges from 0 to 1 on both axes.

pop pop   Ignore the lower left hand corner information, since we know it's zero (that's the default).

newpath   Clear out the current path.

0 1 3 -1 roll div 1 {

This is a loop that steps from *0*, with an increment of *1/number_of_lines* (the number of lines was on the top of the stack; **roll** is used to move it around for dividing it into *1*), up to *1*.

0 0 moveto

1 1 index lineto

Draw a line from *(0, 0)* to *(1, i)*, leaving *i* on the stack (*i* is the index that **for** leaves on the stack).

0 0 moveto 1 lineto

Draw a line from *(0, 0)* to *(i, 1)*, popping *i* off the stack (or rather, using it, and not making a copy to preserve it).

} for

0 0 moveto 1 1 lineto

Draw the diagonal line.

setmatrix

Set the coordinate system back to what it was before we scaled it (the line matrix currentmatrix left the current matrix on the stack).

stroke   Draw the lines. We have to save and restore the current matrix so that when we draw the lines they get the right width.

grestore   Restore the graphics context to what it was before. It is usually good practice for functions to leave the graphics context undisturbed.

} def

10 fanoflines

80

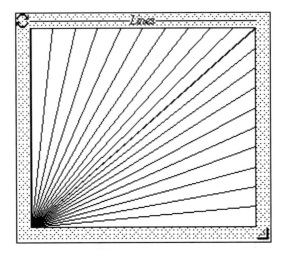

Figure: 4.9.   Graphic output of the fanoflines function.

4.16   NeWS and the PostScript Language

This chapter has reviewed the basics of the standard PostScript language, designed primarily to describe the printed page. The NeWS interpreter stays faithful to the PostScript language definition because compatibility between the printer and the screen is important. Areas where NeWS differs from a PostScript language interpreter for a printer are detailed in Appendix A.

However, NeWS is much more than a PostScript language interpreter; NeWS is a window system. The next chapter explores these extensions.

5
NeWS Facilities for an Interactive World

" I know why there are so many people who love chopping wood.
In this activity one immediately sees the results."

Albert Einstein

5.1   Introduction

The previous chapter described the PostScript language as defined by Adobe Systems, originally designed to drive printers. With printers, only one PostScript program is being executed at a time and output can only take place to a single page at a time. In contrast, NeWS is a window system. It requires that multiple application programs be able to concurrently access the display, which is partitioned into separate regions for each application. And it needs to handle input from a keyboard, a mouse, and the network.

For these added requirements, NeWS incorporates more than the basic PostScript language, adding several facilities to satisfy the demands of an interactive window system environment. For the most part these additions are *completely separate* from the primitives defined by Adobe. The objective in designing the added NeWS facilities was to avoid defining new imaging operators, so that NeWS applications use only standard PostScript operators for output.

The rest of this chapter describes these added facilities. Here are the three most important new types. These new objects are all accessible as new types of PostScript dictionaries, as described in Chapter 4:

canvases   A *canvas* is a drawing surface. Multiple canvases can be displayed and overlapped on the screen. Canvases can be arranged in a hierarchy, and they may be mapped onto other canvases.

processes   A *process* is a thread of execution. NeWS uses what are sometimes called *lightweight* processes. What this means is that a NeWS process is inexpensive to create (in terms of elapsed time, memory usage, and CPU usage) and that all NeWS processes share the same address space.

82

events   *Events* are interprocess messages between lightweight
processes. The keyboard and mouse (and any other input
device) generate events.

Wherever possible, NeWS facilities are patterned after the PostScript language structure. Consistency between the PostScript language and NeWS makes it possible to minimize the number of new operators that have to be defined. For example, many NeWS functions on these new types can be represented as either read or write accesses to fields in the type dictionaries.

Other NeWS facilities are described briefly at the end of this chapter. For a full description of their features, you should read the *NeWS Manual*[SUN87a].

5.2   Canvases

The basic objects a window system manipulates are *windows*. Windows can be thought of as multiple drawing surfaces laid out like sheets of paper on a desktop. Clients of the window system draw on one or more of these windows, and the user moves them around on the desktop, typically bringing the one of the most current interest to the top of the pile.

Canvases are the simple objects that underlie NeWS windows. A NeWS canvas has the properties of an artists canvas: it is an unadorned surface without a frame, to which paint is applied. It is often rectangular, but can in fact be an arbitrary shape. Canvases are arranged in a hierarchy, and a canvas is created on top of its *parent* canvas. Normally, the object that a user thinks of as a window will be made up of several canvases.

5.2.1   The Canvas Structure

A NeWS canvas is a drawing surface. In PostScript language terms, a canvas is a rectangular coordinate space with a boundary defined by a path. Canvases are treated as normal PostScript data objects, and like the current path and the current dictionary, there is the concept of a current canvas. The *current canvas* is part of the current graphics state, and the PostScript graphics operators apply to the current canvas, as they do to the current path. Similarly, the current canvas is saved and restored along with the rest of the state by **gsave/grestore**.

cv **newcanvas** *canvas*
    Creates and returns a canvas whose parent is *cv*.

cv **setcanvas** —

>Makes *cv* be the current canvas. All further graphics
>operations will refer to it.

— **currentcanvas** *cv*

>Returns the current canvas object.

Canvases can be *transparent* or *opaque*. Anything painted on a transparent canvas is actually painted on its parent canvas. A transparent canvas has no real surface of its own, it is actually a piece of another canvas. Transparent canvases are useful for defining areas that are sensitive to input but that do not interfere with drawing in other canvases. Opaque canvases are independent surfaces. An opaque canvas will obscure those parts of other canvases that lie beneath it.

A canvas may also be *retained*, upon request of the client that creates the canvas (such as the window manager). While a canvas is being retained, an off-screen copy of its contents is maintained, and updated as images are drawn into the canvas. If the canvas is moved, or obscured portions of the canvas are exposed, the offscreen copy is automatically moved onto the screen. Retained canvases are more resistant to damage (see Section 5.2.4, Damaged Canvases) and this can improve performance, but retaining can also consume substantial storage particularly on color displays. In light of this, the retained property of a canvas is only a hint; the server may decide at times when memory is scarce to stop retaining a canvas. In general, retained canvases should only be used if it is particularly time-consuming to regenerate the image in the canvas.

A canvas object is actually a dictionary. The internal attributes of the canvas are thus accessible as fields of the canvas dictionary. To set and inspect the values of the various properties of a canvas, the standard dictionary operators can be used.

Creating a sample canvas and setting its properties could thus be done as follows:

```
/cv framebuffer
   newcanvas def
```
>Create a canvas.

```
cv /Transparent false put
```
>Make it opaque.

```
cv /Retained false put
```
>Make it non-retained.

5.2.2   The Canvas Tree

Canvases are arranged in a hierarchical tree structure, the root of which is a device canvas, or the frame buffer itself. The root of the canvas structure is created by using the **createdevice** operator.

string **createdevice** *cv*

> Creates and returns a device canvas. The *string* parameter is interpreted in a system and device dependent manner. For example, on a Sun workstation the string *(/dev/fb)* describes the default frame buffer.

A canvas has some shape and position, whether visible or invisible. If a canvas is to be visible on top of its parent, it must be *mapped*, which is another canvas property. Mapped canvases sit on top of their parent canvases. In effect, there are two separate trees of canvases, one tree containing all canvases descended from a device canvas expressing their familial relationship, and one tree containing only the potentially visible (i.e. mapped) subset of these canvases, expressing their overlapping relationships.

```
/cv framebuffer newcanvas def
```

> Create a child canvas of the framebuffer.

```
cv /Mapped true put
```

> Map it onto the display.

In order for a canvas to be visible on a device, it and all of its ancestors must all be mapped. This hierarchy is used to create what people normally think of as windows: things with borders and titles and scroll bars. For example take figure 5.1.

The various children of a canvas are ordered visually from top to bottom. In Figure 5.1, the frame is the parent of the client's canvas. Assuming all canvases are mapped and opaque, a canvas will obscure (appear to be on top of) its parent, and some of its siblings. The children of a canvas are arranged in a list from lowest to highest, and a canvas will obscure its siblings lower in the list. NeWS provides several operators to manipulate the position of a canvas in relation to its sibling and parent canvases; these operators are used by the NeWS window manager as the user hides and exposes overlapping windowed applications on the screen.

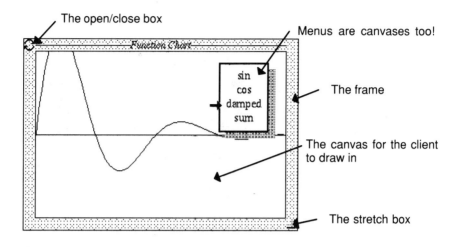

Figure: 5.1.   A window which is built out of four canvases. It has one large canvas
that provides the frame for the window, and three child canvases that
make up the subparts of the window. The window frame is, itself, a
child of a frame buffer canvas.

Examples of canvas manipulation operations are:

cv **canvastobottom** —

> Make canvas *cv* the lowest (least visible) among its siblings.

cv **canvastotop** —

> Make canvas *cv* the highest among its siblings.

S x y **insertcanvasabove** —

> Position the current canvas above one of its siblings *S*, located
> at *(x,y)* relative to its parent.

S x y **insertcanvasbelow** —

> Position the current canvas below one of its siblings *S*.

x y **movecanvas** —

> Position a canvas *cv* at *(x,y)* relative to its parent.

cv **getcanvaslocation** *x y*

> Discover the location of canvas *cv* relative to its parent
> (returns *x y*).

86

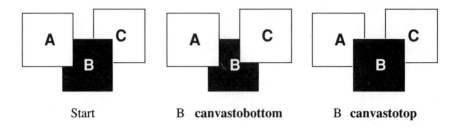

Start   B **canvastobottom**   B **canvastotop**

Figure: 5.2.   Result of two of the operations above — canvastobottom and
                canvastotop.

Note that the position (visibility) of the canvas is not determined by
whether it is the current canvas or not; these two characteristics are entirely
unrelated.

5.2.3 Canvas Shapes

Many window systems restrict their canvases to rectangular shapes, but
NeWS allows canvases to be of any shape that can be described with a path,
even one with holes or disconnected parts.

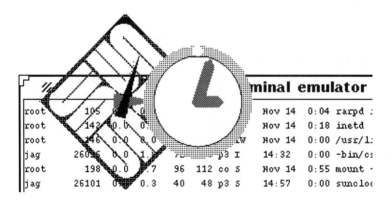

Figure: 5.3.   Non-rectangular canvases: the logo clock & the "round" clock on top
                of the terminal emulator.

cv **reshapecanvas** —

> Sets the shape of *cv* to be the region outlined by the current path. It also sets its default transformation matrix to match the current transformation matrix.

In figure 5.3, the round canvas is defined by a circular path. The code below paraphrases that part of the program that gives the canvas its round shape. We use **psh** to create a canvas, make it round, and give it a coordinate system with the origin in the center of the canvas.

```
shell prompt% psh
```

```
executive
```

Welcome to NeWS Version 1.1

```
/cv framebuffer newcanvas
```

```
def
```
Create a canvas that is a child of the frame buffer.

```
framebuffer setcanvas
```

The current canvas is now the frame buffer.

```
300 300 translate
```

Change the coordinate system so that the origin is where *300,300* used to be.

```
0 0 100 0 360 arc
```

Construct a circular path centered at the origin with radius *100* — remember that the origin has been translated.

```
cv reshapecanvas
```

Reshape the new canvas: it will be circular with the origin of its default coordinate system being in the center of the circle.

```
cv /Mapped true put
```

Make the canvas visible.

```
cv setcanvas
```

Make it be the current canvas. The CTM gets set to the default coordinate system of the canvas, which in this case puts the origin in the center of the canvas.

```
erasepage
```
Fill the canvas with white.

```
0 0 moveto 100 100 lineto stroke
```

Draw a line in the canvas. Notice that it starts in the center of the canvas.

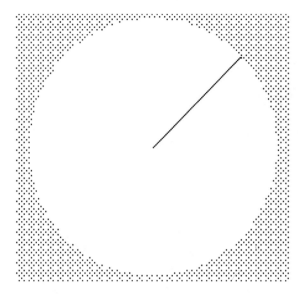

Figure: 5.4.　　The result of the sequence above; a round canvas with a line in it.

The output of a standard PostScript program sent to a printer is clipped to the intersection of the shape of the page and the clip specified in the graphics context, set by the **clip** or **initclip** operator. The analogy in NeWS would be to clip to the intersection of the shape of the canvas and the current graphics state clip path. In fact, NeWS provides one additional clip, a clip that is a property of the canvas rather than the graphics state, and output is clipped to the intersection of all three clips.

clipcanvas　　Set the current canvas' clip to the current path.

clipcanvaspath

　　　　　　Set the current path to the current canvas' clip.

You can see the effect of the canvas clip if we use it to restrict output to the center of the round canvas in the previous example:

```
newpath        Make a new path for the new clip.

0 0 50 0 360 arc
```

　　　　　　Construct a circle centered at the origin with radius 50.

```
clipcanvas     Make the current canvas' clip this path.

0 0 moveto -100 100 lineto stroke
```

　　　　　　Draw a line from the center to the edge of the canvas —
　　　　　　only the center part will be visible.

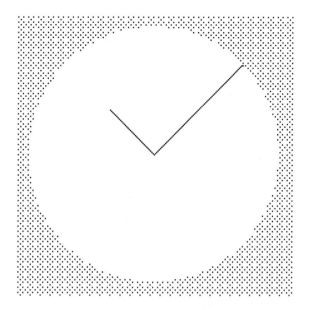

Figure: 5.5.   The result of the sequence above, showing the canvas clip.

The canvas clip is used during damage repair, and at other times when out-put must be restricted to only part of a visible canvas.

To remove the round canvas from the screen, all that is needed is to re-move all the references to it.

```
/cv null def
```

>   Remove the reference from the process' userdict. The
>   canvas will remain on the screen.

```
framebuffer setcanvas
```

>   Remove the reference from the process' graphics state.
>   The canvas will vanish from the screen.

5.2.4 Damaged Canvases

Printed pages never change size and they retain their image no matter how other pages obscure or reveal them in the pile on the desktop. Canvases on a display are not so robust. The image in a canvas can vanish at any time. The canvas can be reshaped, so that the image needs to be rescaled. The canvas can be covered by another canvas, and the window system may not have retained the obscured part of the image in off-screen memory. Retaining canvases con-sumes memory, and there may not be enough memory available when more than a few canvases are displayed on the screen, or if the framebuffer is more than one bit deep.

A canvas is therefore *damaged* when some part of its image is invalid. Damage can happen in many ways. When a canvas is first mapped, its entire visible image is considered damaged (unless it is retained, in which case the whole image is considered damaged when the canvas is created). Any time that an obscured area of a canvas is exposed, by moving away an elder sibling for example, one of two things happens: if the canvas is retained, the saved part of the image is used to fill in the exposed part; if the canvas is not retained, then the exposed part is damaged.

NeWS, like most other window systems, requires its clients to repair any damage that may occur that it can't repair itself. Exactly how a client manages to reconstruct the contents of a damaged part of a canvas is up to that client, but the basic mechanism by which damage is repaired is the same for all. When damage occurs a message is sent to the client program using the event mechanism. The client should eventually respond to the message and repair the damage. If some damage occurs in the intervening time, the record of the damaged area is simply enlarged to include the new damage. It is important to understand that the damage notification message does not include the damage record, which describes the extent of the damage. The client program must explicitly request the damage record from the window system through the **damagepath** operator. This damage communication protocol is used in order to avoid multiple damage repairs by the client. Since the client and the window system may be asynchronous, the damage record is not passed to the client until the window system knows that the client knows that there is damage and can repair all damaged areas.

5.2.5 Canvas Dictionary

Like most of the new types NeWS defines, canvas objects are accessible as dictionaries. The Canvas dictionary has the following fields:

Transparent
> True if the canvases behind show through.

Mapped   True if the canvas is visible.

Retained   True if the invisible parts of the canvas are being preserved in off-screen memory. Retaining canvases helps prevent damage, but does not eliminate it entirely.

SaveBehind
> True if the obscured parts of canvases behind this one are being preserved in off-screen memory. Setting SaveBehind True on transient canvases, such as pop-up menus, helps prevent damage to other canvases, but does not eliminate it entirely.

Initial configuration.

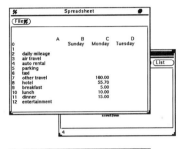

Bottom window gets moved to the top, which sends a damage message off to the client, asking for the region to be redrawn.

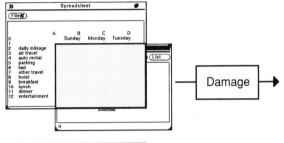

Client replies to damage with commands to redraw the newly exposed parts of the image.

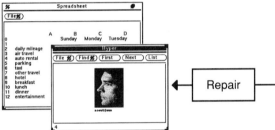

Figure: 5.6.   A damaged window on a screen, with a message going to the client to request repair of the window.

Color   True if the canvas can show colors other than black and white or grayscale.

EventsConsumed

Three possible values, as follows. Events are explained in more detail in Section 5.5.

AllEvents

This canvas prevents any events passing through to those behind.

MatchedEvents

This canvas prevents any events it matches passing through.

NoEvents

This canvas passes all events through to those behind.

All these fields are read-write, and setting them will change the properties of the canvas, except for **Color**, which depends upon the properties of the device on which NeWS is running.

5.2.6   Offscreen Canvases

NeWS also provides facilities to manipulate canvases that are not on a screen. There are two ways to create such canvases.

width height bits/sample matrix proc **buildimage** *cv*

> Constructs an offscreen canvas that is *width* pixels wide and *height* pixels high. Each pixel is *bits/sample* bits deep. The default matrix is specified by *matrix*. *Proc* is executed repeatedly to obtain the initial image data. *Proc* is expected to return a string which contains the pixel values packed into its bytes. The arguments to **buildimage** correspond exactly to the arguments to the standard PostScript **image** operator. As a special case, if *proc* is **null** the image is zeroed.

string **readcanvas** *cv*

file **readcanvas** *cv*

> Constructs an offscreen canvas by reading its contents from the *file* object or from the file named by *string*.

These canvases can be treated, for the most part, like other canvases: they can become the current canvas and you can render into them. But you can't map them to the screen, or do any of the other operations that are particular to screen canvases. There is an operator that will take one canvas and display it on another.

cv **imagecanvas** —

> Renders *cv* onto the current canvas. It is very similar to the standard PostScript **image** operator, except that it gets the image from a canvas object rather that from a user-defined procedure. The standard PostScript **image** operator can be broken into two pieces: one that constructs a canvas, and one that renders it on another canvas. **Image** is exactly equivalent to { **buildimage imagecanvas** }.

5.3   Lightweight Processes

A printer need only do one thing at a time, that is, print on the current page. As a result, the standard PostScript language is a uniprocessing environment. It supports only a single thread of PostScript execution. But in the world of user interfaces, many different processes may be executing simultaneously. Concurrency is required. Luca Cardelli and Rob Pike identify the problem as follows:

> *"Providing a suitable graphical display is not especially difficult;*
> *what causes problems is the complicated flow of control required*
> *to deal with all the possible sequences of user actions with the*
> *input devices."* [CARD85]

Cardelli, Pike, and others have demonstrated how much easier it is to write a consistent user interface as a set of cooperating parallel processes, rather than, for example, a single-threaded, finite state automaton.

NeWS supports parallel processing in the user interface by maintaining a set of processes that each execute independent PostScript programs. UNIX processes are *heavyweight*; they have their own contexts and are expensive in terms of start-up time and consumption of system resources. NeWS processes are said to be *lightweight* because they are inexpensive, easy to create and switch among, and they all share the same address space. The NeWS lightweight processes need no support from the operating system, and are not scheduled by the operating system scheduler. Creating a new NeWS process takes only a few hundred microseconds. Because NeWS lightweight processes are so cheap, they may be used extensively (and are in the Lite toolkit package). For example, each time a menu is invoked, the menu package creates a lightweight process to listen for input in the menu. Lightweight processes communicate through a general interprocess communication (IPC) facility, implemented by *events*, described below. Each individual thread of PostScript interpretation is represented as a process object.

When NeWS is initialized, it creates a single process, or thread, which executes the NeWS start-up file (normally *init.ps*), which may download code into the NeWS server and start up many more lightweight processes. All processes except this first one are the result of earlier processes executing the **fork** operator.

There are quite a few primitives associated with the process mechanism. Here are a few of the most important:

proc **fork** *process*

> Creates a new process that is executing the code in *proc*. When *proc* returns, the process terminates. **fork** returns a process object that may be used to manipulate the process. A newly created process is the *child* process of the *parent* process that created it. When a process starts it is running in an environment that is a clone of its parent process' environment. The dictionary stack, operand stack, and graphics state are copied to the new process.

94

process **waitprocess** *return*

> Waits for *process* to terminate and then returns the value that was on the top of its stack. If its stack is empty when it terminates, *null* is returned.

— **pause** —

> Momentarily suspends the current process, letting other processes execute. Once all other processes that want to run have taken a turn, the current process resumes. This is used for fine-grained control of scheduling.

process **killprocess** —

> Kills (terminates) *process* by causing the *killprocess* error to occur in it.

— **newprocessgroup** —

> Processes can be grouped together. When *fork* is executed, parent and child are in the same process group.
>
> **newprocessgroup** removes the current process from its process group and creates a new process group that contains only the current process.

process **killprocessgroup** —

> Like **killprocess**, except that it kills all processes in the same group as *process*.

  suspendprocess, **breakpoint**, and **continueprocess** are additional commands that help debug the running NeWS process.

  Each lightweight process has complete control over the extent to which its name space is shared with other processes. This sharing is a consequence of the fact that the PostScript language mechanism for resolving references

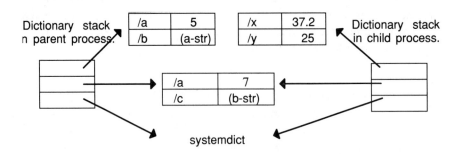

Figure: 5.7.   The dictionary stacks of two processes, one the child of another. They share two dictionaries, but each has a private dictionary on the top of its stack.

to data objects is based on a stack of dictionaries. As discussed in Chapter 4, a dictionary is a table whose key-value elements are pairs of PostScript objects. Each process has a stack of such dictionaries.

Names are bound to values by looking them up in each dictionary, starting from the top of the stack. When a child process is **fork**ed, it inherits a copy of its parent's dictionary stack, so the child process starts with the same name space as its parent. If one process defines a new name in some dictionary in its shared stack, the other will see it.

However, the child process can push and pop dictionaries to and from its private stack, thus controlling the extent that its name space is actually shared with its parent and with other processes.

5.4 Monitors

Whenever a system has asynchronous processes that can share data, some kind of mechanism is needed to keep them from accessing and trying to change the same data at the same time: they need to be synchronized. The PostScript language, having only a single thread of execution, does not need any form of interlock to protect shared write access to data. NeWS, on the other hand, requires some form of interlock to provide processes with consistent access to shared data. It provides monitors for this purpose. A monitor is an object that is restricted to being accessed by at most one process at a time. It is similar to the monitors introduced by Hoare[HOAR78]. There are three primitives that deal with them:

— **createmonitor** *monitor*
>> Creates a new monitor object.

monitor proc **monitor** —
>> Executes the code in *proc* with *monitor* locked (entered).
>> At most one process at a time can have a monitor locked. If a process tries to lock a locked monitor, it is blocked until the process which has it releases it. When *proc* returns or is terminated by an error, the *monitor* is unlocked.

monitor **monitorlocked** *bool*
>> Returns true if *monitor* is locked, false otherwise.

Here is a simple example:

```
/mon createmonitor def
/value 0 def
/increment {
    {
```

```
    mon { /value value 1 add def } monitor
  } fork
} def
```

This defines *mon* to be a monitor object and *value* to be the integer 0. **increment** is defined as a function that creates a process (**fork**) which locks *mon* and, with *mon* locked, increments *value*. So, if we do the following:

increment   Create a process,

increment   create another just like it,

increment   and another.

three processes are created executing in parallel all modifying *value*. Because of the monitor there is no chance of one process modifying *value* while another is doing the same, so the final value of *value* will be three:

value ==   Print out the value of ''value''.

3   Just as we expected.

Of course, since NeWS currently has non-preemptive scheduling and runs on single-processor machines, and since increment doesn't pause, the value would have been three even without the monitor. But in the future, we expect NeWS to implement other scheduling policies, for which the use of monitors will be essential.

5.5   Events

There are three types of communication that take place as NeWS runs. First, as described previously in Chapter 2, and in more detail in Chapter 7, client processes send PostScript byte streams to lightweight PostScript processes within the server. Second, the server receives input from devices, such as the keyboard and locator, and performs output on its display. Third, the NeWS lightweight processes pass messages to each other.

The following diagram shows the communication paths between clients, devices, and the lightweight processes within the server.

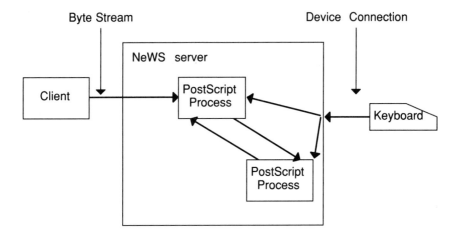

Figure: 5.8.   All of the thick arrows in this drawing indicate communication through events. This is essentially all interprocess communication and all communication from the keyboard and mouse to processes.

Input and communication between lightweight processes are integrated in NeWS through a general interprocess communication mechanism called *events*. Events are NeWS objects which can be generated either by lightweight processes, the server, or by external devices such as the mouse and keyboard. They are received, translated, dispatched, and routed by the server to its PostScript program clients. A process can send an event to itself or any other process, or, it can place an event into the server's event distribution mechanism, in which case it will be distributed just as if it had been generated by an input device.

Event objects can represent one of three things:

1   A message from one lightweight process to another.

2   A description of some event external to all lightweight processes, such as a mouse movement, or damage to a canvas.

3   A template against which other event objects are matched.

In fact, there is no way for a lightweight process receiving an event to tell if it has come from an external event source or from another process; to a receiving process the first two types of event are identical. This allows processes, for example the *NeWScorder* journalling process, to simulate devices and to drive NeWS clients just as a user would.

Events can be thought of as structured objects with a number of fields. As with canvases and processes, these fields are accessed as if the event were a dictionary and the fields were keys in that dictionary. Most of these fields are mentioned as they become relevant in this section. Among the most interesting fields in an event are:

/**Name**   The name of an event, it describes what happened. For instance, it may be an integer ASCII character or keystation code. Or it may be a keyword describing an abstract operation like /**AcceptFocus** or /**DeSelect**.

/**Action**   A modifier for the name field. It usually describes what happened to the named thing. For instance, keyboard characters usually have an action of either /**DownTransition** or /**UpTransition**.

/**TimeStamp**

The time when an event happened. Events are delivered strictly in order of their time stamp. No two events can have the same timestamp.

/**Canvas**   The canvas that the event "happened in" or is "directed to". The keyboard and the mouse typically set this to the uppermost canvas that was under the cursor when the event happened.

5.5.1   Events as Templates

Internal interprocess events are used in two ways, as messages that are sent to processes, and as templates that a process uses to describe the events in which it is interested. A process specifies the kinds of events it would like to receive by constructing events that look like these interesting events, and expressing interest in them. These template events are called *interests,* and as real events occur they are *matched* against these templates. Events that match correctly will eventually be received by the process that expressed the interest.

Here are the most important of the event primitives:

— **createevent** *event*

Creates a blank event. All of its fields are null (when used in an interest event, null matches anything).

event **sendevent** —

Sends *event* to all the processes that are interested in it.

— **awaitevent** *event*

Returns the next event sent to this process.

event **expressinterest** —

> Expresses interest in *event*. Further events that are generated which match it will be sent to this process. Note: if a process forks its children do not inherit its interests).

event **revokeinterest** —

> Undoes an expression of interest.

event **redistributeevent**—

> Sends *event* (which must have been received by **awaitevent**) back to the distribution process to see if any other interest might match it. Normally, when an event is sent it is received by all processes that expressed interest in it. This can be controlled by using the **/Exclusivity** and **/Priority** fields of an interest event.

5.5.2   Event Distribution

Input events enter the system as they are generated by the NeWS server or when a lightweight process executes **sendevent** or **redistributeevent**. Events generated by the server are stamped with the time of their creation; other events are given whatever time stamp is left by the process that sends them (a process can use **currenttime** or **lasteventtime** to generate suitable values). In any case, newly created events are sorted into a single event queue according to their time-stamp values.

Events are removed from the head of the event queue one at a time as the server schedules processes to be run. No event will be distributed before the time indicated in its time stamp. Copies of events are distributed to all processes whose interests it matches and each of those processes is given a chance to run before the next event is taken from the queue.

A process gets its next input event by executing *awaitevent*. If no event has been distributed to it, the process will block. If a distributed event is waiting, *awaitevent* will return immediately with the new event on the top of the operand stack.

5.5.3   Event Matching

No process wants to receive *all* the events that appear on the event queue. Processes determine the events they will receive by constructing an event that looks like an event they would like to receive, and expressing interest in events that look like this template. Real events are matched against these interest templates and, if they match, they are delivered to the process that expressed interest.

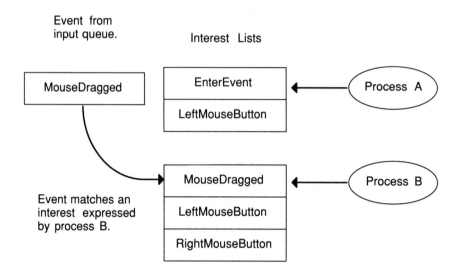

Figure: 5.9.   Events are removed from the queue, matched against interest templates, and distributed to the processes that expressed the interests.

The matching process compares the following fields of the interest and real event:

Name and **Action**. These fields are matched in the same ways according to the following rules:

1   Null in an interest field matches anything in the corresponding field of the real event.

2   If the value in the interest and the value in the real event are the same, the match for that field succeeds. Typically, this will be the case for simple values like booleans, keywords, or numbers.

3   An array or a dictionary in the interest field specifies a class of values the real event may match. A real event value matches if it is any of the elements of the array, or keys in the dictionary.

A null canvas matches events happening anywhere. If the **Canvas** field of the interest is non-null, the match succeeds if the event happened when that canvas was the current input focus, or if the event was sent with a matching canvas field (as, for example, a *Damaged* event for that canvas).

The **Process** field of an interest is set by **expressinterest** to the process expressing the interest. Normally, events being distributed have null in their process fields and will be matched against interests without restriction. If an event has a specific process in its **Process** field, the event will only match interests that have been expressed by that process. It must still match the interest on **Name**, **Action** and **Canvas**.

If all the matching conditions are met, the event matches the interest.

Here's a simple example. We create a process listening for /Hello events, and printing them out. Then we create and send a /Hello event, and the listener prints it out:

```
{                       Start defining a listener process.
   createevent dup begin
                        Create and open an event to be a template.
      /Name /Hello def
                        Listen for /Hello events.
   end expressinterest
                        Express interest in /Hello events.
   { awaitevent == } loop
                        Print out each event as it arrives.
} fork          Fork the listener process.
createevent dup begin
                        Create and open an event to send.
   /Name /Hello def
                        Make it a /Hello event.
   /Action /Mumble def
                        With Action /Mumble.
end sendevent
                        Send the /Hello event.
                        The listener process will wake up and print it.
event(0x3A7E44, [0,0], name(/Hello), action(/Mumble))
createevent dup begin
                        Create and open an event to send.
   /Name /Goodbye def
                        Make it a /Goodbye event.
   /Action /Mumble def
```

102

With Action /Mumble.

```
end sendevent
```

Send the /Goodbye event.

No-one is listening for /Goobye events, so nothing happens.

`killprocess` Kill off the listener process — its process object has been on the stack all this time.

5.5.4 Special Events

The NeWS server autonomously generates a number of different input events in response to external events, but unlike many other window systems NeWS events are of only one type. They are distinguished by the values of the fields in the event dictionary. Keystrokes generally have numeric values in their **Name**, but most others are identified by a keyword in the **Name**. The most important of these keywords are:

Damaged   Generated for a canvas whenever it is damaged. The total damage is accessible with **damagepath**. The **Action** for a damage event is null, and the **Canvas** field identifies the affected canvas.

EnterEvent & ExitEvent
            When the cursor is moved across a border between canvases, multiple events are generated. In each event, the **Name** is either **EnterEvent** or **ExitEvent**, depending on the direction of the crossing. The **Action** field contains a more detailed description between the canvas and the cursor.

MouseDragged, LeftMouseButton, MiddleMouseButton
&RightMouseButton
            Manipulation of the mouse generates events with these names. If the mouse moves, the event **Name** is **MouseDragged** and the **Action** is null. If a mouse button is pressed or released, the **Name** identifies which button is affected and the **Action** is one of the keywords **DownTransition** or **UpTransition**.

As an example of the use of interests, the round canvas used earlier is created and a line is drawn from the center to the place where the left mouse button is clicked:

```
% psh
```

```
executive
```

Welcome to NeWS Version 1.1

```
/cv framebuffer newcanvas
```

```
def
```
Create a canvas that is a child of the frame buffer.

```
framebuffer setcanvas
```
The current canvas is now the frame buffer.

```
300 300 translate
```
Change the coordinate system so that the origin is where *300,300* used to be.

```
0 0 100 0 360 arc
```
Construct a circle centered at the origin with radius *100* — remember that the origin has been translated.

```
cv reshapecanvas
```
Reshape the new canvas: it will be circular with the origin of its default coordinate system being in the center of the circle.

```
cv /Mapped true put
```
Make the canvas visible.

```
cv setcanvas
```
Make it be the current canvas. The CTM gets set to the default coordinate system of the canvas, which in this case puts the origin in the center of the canvas.

```
erasepage
```
Fill the canvas with white.

```
{
```
Start defining a procedure that will eventually be forked as a process printing out each event.

```
createevent dup begin
```
Create an event to serve as an interest, leave a reference to it on the stack, and push the event on the dictionary stack.

```
/Canvas cv def
```
Set the Canvas field of the interest to the round canvas, indicating that we're interested only in events in the canvas.

```
/Name /LeftMouseButton def
```

```
/Action /UpTransition def
```
Set the Name and Action fields of the interest, indicating

that we're interested only in up transitions of the left mouse button.

```
end expressinterest
```

Pop the interest off the dictionary stack, and use the reference to it on the stack to express interest in events that match it.

```
{ awaitevent == } loop
```

Loop forever, printing out each event that arrives.

```
} fork
```

Take the procedure we've defined and make a process running it.

Now, left-click once in the round canvas, and the process forked prints the event describing the click. Try clicking the other mouse buttons, and clicking the left button outside the round canvas. Notice that nothing happens. These events don't match the interest.

event(0x47FAB8, [435,467], name(/LeftMouseButton), action(/UpTransition), canvas(201x201@300,400))

Next, we replace the printout process by one drawing a line to the click:

```
killprocess
```
Destroy the printing process.

```
{
```
Start defining a procedure that will eventually be forked as a process drawing lines in the canvas.

```
createevent dup begin
```

Create an event to serve as an interest, leave a reference to it on the stack, and push the event on to the dictionary stack.

```
/Canvas cv def
```

Set the Canvas field of the interest to the round canvas, indicating that we're interested only in events in the canvas.

```
/Name /LeftMouseButton def
/Action /UpTransition def
```

Set the Name and Action fields of the interest, indicating that we're interested only in up transitions of the left mouse button.

```
end expressinterest
```

Pop the interest off the dictionary stack, and use the reference to it on the stack to express interest in events that match it.

```
{                     Start defining what we will do on each event.
```

```
    awaitevent begin
```

Wait until we get an event, then push it on the dictionary stack so that we can access its fields.

```
        0 0 moveto
```

Start the line at the center of the canvas.

```
    XLocation YLocation lineto stroke
```

End the line at the click, and stroke it out.

```
        end
```
Finished with the event, so pop it off the dictionary stack.

```
      } loop
```
Finish defining what we do on every event.

```
} fork
```
Take the procedure we've defined and make a process running it.

Now, left-click in the round canvas, and the process forked draws a line from the center of the canvas to the mouse position for each click. Once again, note that other buttons have no effect.

Remember to kill off the process drawing the lines and remove the references from the **psh** process. If you don't the round canvas will remain after you exit from the **psh**.

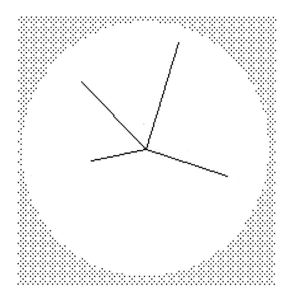

Figure: 5.10.   The results of the example, a round canvas with lines where we clicked.

```
killprocess
```
Destroy the line-drawing process and its references to the round canvas.

```
/cv null def
```
Remove the reference from the **psh** process' userdict.

```
framebuffer setcanvas
```
Remove the reference from the psh process' graphics state.

This is explained in the section below on storage management.

There are no special timer events in NeWS; rather, the guarantee that no event will be delivered from the event queue before the time in its time stamp means that any event can be used to generate another event at some time in the future. There is no requirement that a process send a timer event to itself; it can just as easily send a delayed message to another process, or broadcast one, by changing the Process field in the event passed to **sendevent**.

Here is an example program using this capability. It ticks, printing out a new event every 12 seconds (0.2 of a minute — times in NeWS are in minutes and fractions):

```
{
```
Start defining a procedure that will eventually be forked as a ticking process.

```
    createevent dup begin
```
Create an event to serve as an interest, leave a reference to it on the stack, and push the event on the dictionary stack.

```
    /Name /Hello def
```
Set the Name field to show that we're interested in /Hello events.

```
    end expressinterest
```
Pop the interest off the dictionary stack, and use the reference to it on the stack to express interest in events that match it.

```
    {
```

```
    awaitevent ==
```
Print out each event as it arrives.

```
    createevent dup begin
```
Create and open the next event.

```
    /Name /Hello def
```

Make it a /Hello event.

```
/TimeStamp currenttime 0.2 add def
```

Make the timestamp 12 seconds in the future.

```
    end sendevent
```

And send it to be delivered in 12 seconds.

```
  } loop
```
Loop for ever.

```
} fork
```
Take the procedure we've defined and make a process running it.

Nothing happens until we send an event to start.

```
createevent dup begin
```

Create an event to be the trigger.

```
    /Name /Hello def
```

Make it a /Hello event.

```
end sendevent
```

And send it — it gets printed immediately.

event(0x1FA12C, [0,0], name(/Hello), action(null))

12 seconds later, we get another.

event(0x1FA280, [0,0], name(/Hello), action(null))

And 12 seconds later, another.

event(0x205590, [0,0], name(/Hello), action(null))

```
killprocess
```
Kill off the listener process.

5.5.5   Processing After a Match

After a real event has been successfully matched with an interest, a copy of the event is made and eventually delivered. In effect, event distribution is a broadcast mechanism; all processes interested in an event see a copy of that event. In this broadcast copy, the **Interest** field is set to the interest matched, and the **Process** and **Canvas** fields to the process and canvas of that interest. If the **Name** and/or **Action** values matched a key in a dictionary in the corresponding field in the interest, one of two things will happen:

If the value in the dictionary corresponding to the matching key is not
executable, then the value replaces the **Name** or **Action** field in the event.

108

If the dictionary value is executable, then the value in the corresponding
field of the event is not modified; instead, the executable object from the
dictionary is queued for execution in the receiving process immediately
after the event is returned by **awaitevent**. If both the **Name** and **Action**
fields of the event have such executable matches the **Name** is executed
first, then the **Action**.

The replacement of the **Name** or **Action** fields can be demonstrated with
a simple example that listens for /Ping events and maps them into /Pong
events, and vice versa. This could be used, for example, to map function
keys into strings:

```
{
```
> Start defining a procedure that will eventually be forked
> as a listener process.

```
    createevent dup begin
```
> Create an event to serve as an interest, leave a reference to
> it on the stack, and push the event on the dictionary stack.

```
        2 dict dup begin
```
> Create a dictionary for the name field.

```
            /Ping /Pong def
```
> Turn a /Ping into a /Pong.

```
            /Pong /Ping def
```
> Turn a /Pong into a /Ping.

```
        end /Name exch def
```
> Put the dict in the Name field to show that we're
> interested in /Ping & /Pong events.

```
    end expressinterest
```
> Pop thc interest off the dictionary stack, and use the
> reference to it on the stack to express interest in events
> that match it.

```
    { awaitevent == } loop
```
> Print the events we receive.

```
} fork
```
> Take the procedure we've defined and make a process
> running it.

```
createevent dup begin
```
> Create an event.

```
    /Name /Ping def
```
> Make it a /Ping event.

```
end sendevent
```

> And send it — we get a `/Pong`.

`event(0x2035C0, [0,0], name(/Pong), action(null))`

```
createevent dup begin
```

> Create an event.

```
   /Name /Pong def
```

> Make it a `/Pong` event.

```
end sendevent
```

> And send it — we get a `/Ping`.

`event(0x1DBDF8, [0,0], name(/Ping), action(null))`

`killprocess` Kill off the listener process.

The executable match process can be demonstrated by attaching code to the interest:

```
{
```

> Start defining a procedure that will eventually be forked as a listener process.

```
   createevent dup begin
```

> Create an event to serve as an interest, leave a reference to it on the stack, and push the event on the dictionary stack.

```
   2 dict dup begin
```

> Create a dictionary for the name field.

```
   /Ping { (Ping) == } def
```

> Print Ping when a `/Ping` event is matched.

```
   /Pong { (Pong) == } def
```

> Print Pong when a `/Pong` event is matched.

```
   end /Name exch def
```

> Put the dict in the Name field to show that we're interested in `/Ping` & `/Pong` events.

```
   end expressinterest
```

> Pop the interest off the dictionary stack, and use the reference to it on the stack to express interest in events that match it.

```
{ awaitevent pop } loop
```

> Do nothing with the events we receive. The executable match code in the `/Name` dict will be run before the pop.

110

```
} fork
```
Take the procedure we've defined and make a process running it.

```
createevent dup begin
```
Create an event.

```
  /Name /Ping def
```
Make it a /Ping event.

```
end sendevent
```
And send it.

(Ping) The executable match prints Ping.

```
createevent dup begin
```
Create an event.

```
  /Name /Pong def
```
Make it a /Pong event.

```
end sendevent
```
And send it.

(Pong) The executable match prints Pong.

```
killprocess
```
Kill off the listener process.

Once the copy has been received, it is placed on a private queue for the process that expressed the interest. If that process was blocked in **awaitevent**, it is made runnable. The original event then may be matched against further interests.

This processing of the **Name** and **Action** fields is a generalization of the concept of *keymapping* supported by many window systems. Every time an event is received, it can potentially be processed not merely by a dictionary lookup and replacement, but even by a PostScript procedure specific to that individual key. The procedure can be specified by some process other than the one receiving the events.

5.6   Color

The PostScript language as specified has a very simple color model. There are two primitives, **sethsbcolor** and **setrgbcolor** used to specify the color of subsequent fill operations. NeWS extends this concept by adding special color objects and some primitives to manipulate them.

r g b **rgbcolor** *color*

> Returns a color object whose red, green and blue components are set to *r*, *g*, and *b*.

h s b **hsbcolor** *color*

> Returns a color object whose red, green, and blue components are calculated from the hue, saturation, and brightness values, *h*, *s*, and *b*.

color **setcolor** —

> Sets the current color to *color*.

— **currentcolor** *color*

> Returns the current color.

So the sequence *rgbcolor* **setcolor** is equivalent to **setrgbcolor**, and *hsbcolor* **setcolor** is equivalent to **sethsbcolor**. For both *hsbcolor* and *rgbcolor*, the same color object will be returned if the same arguments are given. Colors can thus be compared using the normal PostScript **eq** operator. The color that actually appears on the screen is only an approximation to these values, and several sets of RGB or HSB values may end up mapping to the same color on the screen. The **contrastswithcurrent** operator detects if a color *color* will be distinguishable from the current color.

color **contrastswithcurrent** *bool*

> Returns True or False.

5.7   Storage Management

The PostScript language was designed for printers with limited amounts of memory running "one-shot" programs, and could, therefore, take a somewhat idiosyncratic approach to storage management. The **save** operator remembers a state of (most of) a PostScript program's memory in a *save* object, and the **restore** operator restores the state of (most of) the memory to that of the save object.

This approach cannot survive in a multiprocess world, where objects are shared between processes, so NeWS uses reference counts on objects, and garbage collection. Objects persist as long as at least one reference to them exists. When the last reference goes away, the object vanishes and its space is reclaimed. NeWS programmers need to be careful not to let processes place references to private data objects in shared dictionaries; the private objects will persist after the process dies. A common example is accidentally using **def** to place a reference to a canvas into **systemdict** rather than a private dictionary. When the process dies a zombie canvas remains behind.

In the preceeding example, in which a process was forked off to listen to mouse clicks and draw a line for each it receives, it's important to remember to kill off the process. If you don't, it will remain active and it will retain its reference to the canvas it has created. It will be effectively stuck on the screen since the process doesn't listen for any termination commands.

Garbage collection in NeWS is intended to be invisible, and has almost no impact on a PostScript program or the language itself. The PostScript language contains primitives for creating objects, but none for releasing them. This structure lends itself naturally to a garbage collector that releases objects when they are no longer referenced. A reference count garbage collector is simple and evenly distributes the cost of doing garbage collection throughout the execution of the server. Most other garbage collectors either double the amount of memory used, or occasionally pause for a long time to sweep memory and collect garbage. Neither of these side-effects were considered acceptable.

5.8   Debugging in NeWS

The PostScript language offers very few debugging facilities, at least partly because it is often difficult to get access to what is happening inside a printer. A major problem in printer debugging is that the only connection to the outside world is already being used for sending data to be printed. NeWS, being a multiprocess interpreter intended for an interactive environment, requires a more sophisticated debugging environment and runs on platforms that are better able to support debugging facilities. NeWS supports an interactive, multiprocess debugger with which one can perform both breakpoint and post-mortem debugging of any number of lightweight NeWS processes.

In order to use the debugger the following command should be entered:

```
(NeWS/debug.ps) run
```

This instruction can also be included in the user-tailorable *user.ps* startup file. Once the debugger has been started, one or more interactive connections to it can be set up by invoking **psh** as described in Chapter 4 and typing the following:

```
executive
dbgstart
```

Now, whenever a lightweight process gets an error, it will stop and a message describing the error will appear in all these interactive debugger connections. In any of the interactive debuggers other commands, detailed in the NeWS manual, can be used to:

Examine the state of any of the stopped processes.

Add breakpoints to procedures.

Add debugging printout commands to procedures.

Execute PostScript procedures in the context of any of the stopped process.

Restart any of the stopped processes.

```
              } loop
} fork
createevent dup begin
        /Name /Hello def
end sendevent
event(0x2442A0, [0,0], name(/Hello), action(null))
```

```
                                        h19 terminal emulator
devnull% psh
executive
Welcome to NeWS Version 1.1
(NeWS/debug.ps) run
dbgstart
Debugger installed.
Break: undefined from process(10227720, input_wait)
currently pending breakpoints are:
    1: undefined called from process(10227720, input_wait)
```

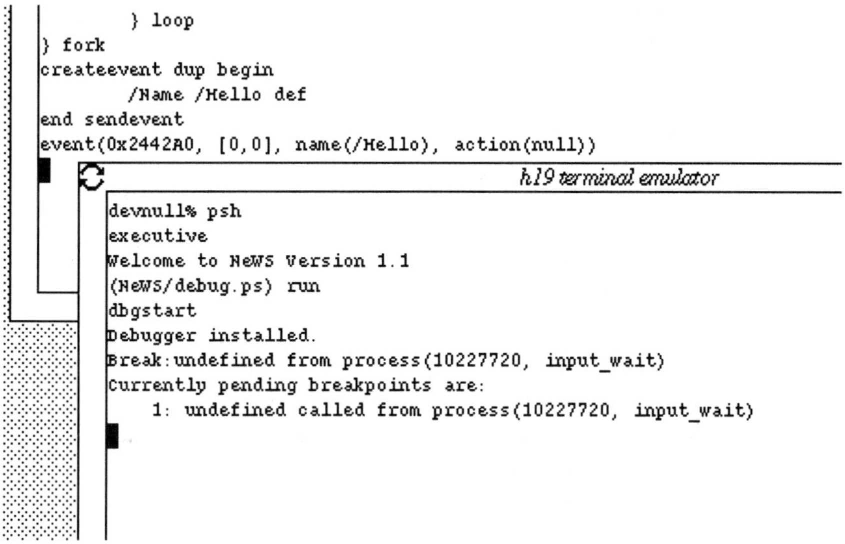

Figure: 5.11.   The debugger on the screen.

This structure, with multiple interactive connections to a single central debugger, seems odd at first sight. But, in a multi-process environment, the ability to examine both sides of an interaction between two processes is essential, and this framework allows the user to freely assign interactive contexts to processes as it becomes convenient.

The simplest use of the debugger is to trap processes that cause errors. To illustrate this, we need two interactive connections (see Figure 5.11). In one, we type a program with an error, and in the other we communicate with the debugger.

Into the first session, we mis-type the earlier repeating event example:

{   Start defining a procedure that will eventually be forked
                as a ticking process.

```
createevent dup begin
```

114

Create an event to serve as an interest, leave a reference to
it on the stack, and push the event on the dictionary stack.

```
/Name /Hello def
```

Set the Name field to show that we're interested in
/Hello events.

```
end expressinterest
```

Pop the interest off the dictionary stack, and use the
reference to it on the stack to express interest in events
that match it.

```
{
```

```
awaitevent ==
```

Print out each event as it arrives.

```
createevent dup begin
```

Create and open the next event.

```
/Name /Hello def
```

Make it a /Hello event.

```
/TimeStamp currentime 0.2 add def
```

Make the timestamp 12 seconds in the future. Notice that
currenttime has been misspelled. This is the bug we are
looking for.

```
end sendevent
```

And send it to be delivered in 12 seconds.

```
} loop
```
Loop forever.

```
} fork
```
Take the procedure we've defined and make a process
running it.

Nothing happens until we send an event to start.

```
createevent dup begin
```

Create an event to be the trigger.

```
/Name /Hello def
```

Make it a /Hello event.

```
end sendevent
```

And send it — it gets printed immediately, and then we
hit the bug.

event(0x1FA12C, [0,0], name(/Hello), action(null))

When the listening process that we created to print out the events tries to execute the misspelled **currenttime** primitive, it gets an undefined error. During the process of installing the debugger, it installed its own **error-dict** that traps into the debugger. The result in the debugger connection is:

```
Break:undefined from process(11404420, input_wait)
```

```
Currently pending breakpoints are:
    1: undefined called from process(11404420,
            input_wait)
```

Now, the buggy process is stopped and we can use the debugger to examine it. First, we can find out where the error occurred by printing the execution stack:

dbgwhere   Print the execution stack of the stopped process.

Level 1

```
{ 'awaitevent' '==' 'createevent' 'dup' 'begin'
        Name Hello 'def'

    TimeStamp *currentime 0.2 'add' 'def' 'end'
        'sendevent' } (*9,15)
```

Level 0

```
{ 'createevent' 'dup' 'begin' Name Hello 'def' 'end'
        'expressinterest'

    array{15} *'loop' } (*9,10)
```

The asterix shows the current primitive at each level. The two numbers in parentheses are the zero-based index in the procedure of the current primitive, and the length of the procedure. The "array{15}" in the level 0 procedure is the level 1 procedure.

Next, we print out the stack of the buggy process. We do this by "entering" the stopped process, making the operand and dictionary stacks of the debugging process the same as the buggy process, and allowing us to use the normal PostScript primitives to examine its state:

dbgenter   Enter the context of the stopped process.

pstack   Print out its operand stack.

```
event(0x1FA12C, [0,0], name(/Hello), action(null))
        /TimeStamp currentime
```

The misspelled primitive is on the top of the operand stack. We can replace it with the value that should have been its result, and copy the modified stack back into the buggy process by:

```
pop currenttime pstack
```

> Replace the "curentime" on the stack by the current time, and print the stack.

event(0x1FA12C, [0,0], name(/Hello), action(null))
/TimeStamp 202.0283

```
dbgcopystack
```

> Replace the stack of the stopped process by the copy of it the debugger has been using.

Now the buggy process' stack is correct, we can replace the misspelled primitive in the executable array that contains the bug using **dbgpatch**:

```
1 9 /currenttime load dbgpatch
```

> Overwrite the erroneous primitive in the code that the buggy process is running.

Result: Level 1

Level 1

```
{ 'awaitevent' '==' `createevent' 'dup' 'begin'
        Name Hello 'def'

  TimeStamp *`currenttime' 0.2 'add' 'def' 'end'
        `sendevent' } (*9,15)
```

The numbers 1 and 9 are the execution level, and the index within the executable array at that level. Note the use of **load** to get the value of **currenttime** rather than the word **currenttime** (as we would from **/currenttime**) or the result of executing **currenttime**.

Finally, we leave the buggy process' context, and leave it to execute, by:

```
dbgexit
```
Detach the debugger from the context of the buggy process.

```
dbgcontinue
```
Resume executing the no-longer buggy process.

> Now, in the first psh session, the events start printing out as they should have.

event(0x1FA12C, [0,0], name(/Hello), action(null))

> And, 12 seconds later .....

event(0x1FA12C, [0,0], name(/Hello), action(null))

```
killprocess
```
Kill the ticking process.

As well as these capabilities for repairing broken processes, the debugger provides the ability to set breakpoints, to cause entry and/or exit of a procedure to generate debugging printout, and to add a prelude and a postscript to an existing procedure. It does not, yet, provide for single-stepping stopped processes.

5.9   Next, Writing Interactive Programs

Although, as we have described, NeWS provides a debugger, it is much better not to write bugs in the first place than to have to use it. In the next chapter, we show how an object-oriented style of writing NeWS programs can make it easy to compose interactive applications from pre-defined, tested pieces without needing to be aware of the details of the underlying primitives we have described in this chapter.

6
Object-Oriented PostScript

" If we cannot now end our differences, at least we can help make the
world safe for diversity."

John Fitzgerald Kennedy

The previous chapter introduced the extensions that NeWS makes to the
PostScript language in order to support interaction with a window system.
This chapter shows how these extensions are combined with a stylized way
of writing PostScript programs to make developing interactive programs
easy. We do this by following the gradual construction of a simple example
NeWS client.

6.1   The NeWS Style of Writing PostScript Programs

Some window systems attempt to enforce a consistent style of user interface across all the applications that use them. The Andrew and Macintosh
window systems are good examples. Others, such as SunWindows and the X
window system, attempt only to provide low-level mechanisms, and avoid
specifying any details of the appearance or function of an application's user
interface.

Nevertheless, vendors supplying base window systems like SunWindows
and X do not expect every application to hand craft its user interface from
scratch. They normally provide a layer above the base window system that
implements common components of a user interface such as menus, scroll
bars, buttons and text panels. This upper layer provides a user interface
toolkit; a user interface can be rapidly assembled by selecting and compos-
ing components from the toolkit.

As experience has been gained with these toolkits, much attention has
been focused on toolkits with an *object-oriented* structure and programmer
interface. Object-oriented toolkits allow application developers to selectively customize certain aspects of toolkit components, while still working
within the standard toolkit framework. Applications can take a generic
object from the toolkit, such as a menu, and tailor its appearance or behavior for that application only and not affect other applications. Customizing
for a specific need does not require detailed understanding of the toolkit
internals. Applications can be customized by creating *sub-classes* of generic

object classes. These sub-classed objects inherit all aspects of their generic object subclasses, except for those which the application developer chooses to selectively replace. The freedom to replace or restrict individual aspects of a generic object in an application-specific subclass allows developers to specify only the details in which they have particular interest, and automatically have consistent behaviors for all other aspects of their tailored user interface components.

This evolution towards object-orientation is visible in the history of many existing toolkits. Sun's SunView toolkit has evolved gradually from a conventional subroutine package towards a more object-oriented interface, the major change being from routines with many individual arguments to a single argument, which is a list of attribute-value pairs. This change illustrates the problems of grafting an object-oriented interface onto a language (SunView is written in C) that does not naturally support it. The best popular example of a user interface toolkit designed from the start to be object-oriented is the Macintosh MacApp toolkit. There, a fundamental design decision was to use an object-oriented programming language, Object Pascal.

Many of the essential ideas in object-oriented systems can be mapped to similar constructs in the traditional "package" or "module" based systems:

Packages (modules) are replaced by *classes*.

Procedures in packages are replaced by *methods* in classes.

Creating package objects is replaced by creating new *instances* of a class.

Package local and global variables are replaced by *class variables*.

Object variables are replaced by *instance variables*.

Object-oriented systems also incorporate new ideas that do not correspond to more traditional approaches. Classes are ordered into a hierarchy by *subclassing* a new class from a prior one, *inheriting* its methods, instance variables, and class variables. Means exist to construct these sub-classes dynamically. Few languages can create modules at run-time. Methods are invoked by use of the **send** primitive. The term *message* is used for an invocation of a method with its arguments; send the message "display yourself" to a menu object with the location as a parameter, and the menu's "display yourself" method is executed.

Two new concepts, the *self* and *super* pseudo-variables, are also introduced. They are used when writing the methods of a class to refer to:

self — the object that received the message. To invoke another method of
    the same object, send the message to self.

super — the class's superclass. To invoke a method from the superclass that
    is being overridden in the subclass, send the message to super.

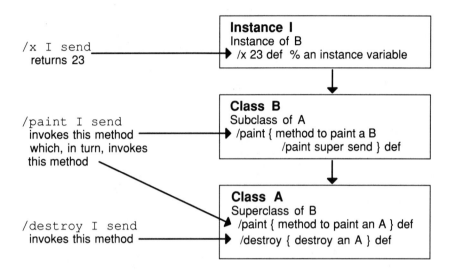

Figure: 6.1.   Class object-oriented relationships showing instance, class, and superclass.

Thus, when writing a method of a class, *self* represents the object in the class that received the message that caused this method to be invoked. *Super* represents the object that received the message as it *would have been* had it been an instance of the superclass, rather than the class being written.

6.1.1   Object-Oriented PostScript Language Programming

NeWS provides mechanisms to encourage an object-oriented style of programming, using concepts and techniques, invented by Owen Densmore, that are implemented entirely in PostScript code within the server. NeWS provides classes, represented as dictionaries containing procedures implementing the methods of the class, and instances of a class, represented as dictionaries containing the instance variables of the class and all its superclasses[DENS86].

When writing applications, you can use these mechanisms in two ways. You can create, assemble, and manipulate objects in pre-defined classes. You can create new subclasses and create objects in these new classes.

To use a pre-defined class, you must send it messages it understands. You send a message to an object with the send operator:

meth obj **send** —

> Invoke the *meth* method of the object *obj.* Any parameters the method needs will be taken from the stack.

NeWS provides some extra flexibility in using pre-defined classes. Unlike most object-oriented language environments, it is not restricted to operating on an object using the methods defined for it by its class. You can provide a new method for an existing object at any time simply by sending the code for the method to the object by:

proc obj **send** —

> Execute *proc* as if it had been defined as a method of the
> object *obj*. Any parameters the method needs will be
> taken from the stack.

If the *meth* argument to a send is an executable array, it is executed in the context of the object exactly as if it had been pre-defined as a method of the object, given a name, and that name supplied as the *meth* argument. This technique is frequently used in NeWS, and the examples below show several uses.

6.1.2   The Lite Toolkit

NeWS uses this implementation of object-oriented programming to provide a user interface toolkit, the Lite toolkit, that allows applications to create and use windows, menus and other user interface objects without knowing the details of their implementation. In particular, the Lite toolkit provides a basic class *Object*, and some important subclasses that are used to construct all Lite user interface components:

Window   The Window class is what clients use instead of a bare canvas
as a surface to draw on. It includes methods for re-sizing, re-
positioning, closing into an icon, opening, and so on.

Menu   Menus associate keys with actions. Keys are objects that can be
drawn, generally a string but possibly a PostScript procedure.
Actions are normally a PostScript procedure, but can possibly
be another menu.

Item   Items are user-definable graphic interactive objects, such as a
button, a slider, or a scroll bar.

These classes have variables pointing to a default implementation, for example DefaultWindow. It starts out being the LiteWindow class. All applications using the DefaultWindow will look the same, that is, like a LiteWindow. You can create a new window class, perhaps called MyWindow, and set DefaultWindow to point to it. Now all the subsequent windows you create will look like a MyWindow.

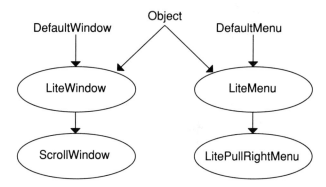

Figure: 6.2.   Part of the Lite toolkit object hierarchy.

The remainder of this chapter describes the construction of a simple NeWS client, using each of these pre-defined classes in turn, and then by creating new subclasses.

6.2   Class Window

Almost all NeWS clients will want a canvas on which to draw their image. They normally get one by creating a new instance of class *Default-Window*. New objects are created by sending the message *new* to the object representing their class.

shell prompt% psh

executive

Welcome to NeWS Version 1.1

/win   Put *win* on the stack for later use.

framebuffer The parent of *win* is the framebuffer.

/new DefaultWindow send

Make a new instance of the *DefaultWindow* class by sending the new message to the class object.

def   Call it *win*. It will not appear until it is mapped.

Clients will then ask the user to specify the size and location of the new Window using a rubber-band box interaction, and make the new Window visible with these parameters:

```
/reshapefromuser win send
```
Set size and location of *win* from the user.

```
/map win send
```
Make window visible by invoking method */map*.

Figure: 6.3.   On screen version of a default instance of LiteWindow.

Although the default window appears simple, it has many interesting characteristics. It can overlay other windows and be overlaid by them. It has a border with window controls in the top-left and bottom-right corners. Left-clicking on the circular icon in the top-left corner closes the window into an icon.

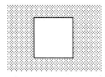

Figure: 6.4.   Default LiteWindow icon.

Press the right button in the icon and the default icon menu appears. Selecting "'Open'' from the menu re-opens the window.

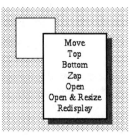

Figure: 6.5.   Default LiteWindow icon menu.

125

Grabbing the bottom-right control with the left button and dragging it causes the window to be resized.

Grabbing the border with the middle mouse button drags the whole window to a new position. Clicking the left mouse button pops the window to the top of the hierarchy of windows so it is completely visible. Pressing the right mouse button in the border pops-up a menu of generic window operations such as Move and Resize.

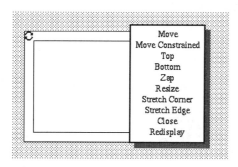

Figure: 6.6.   The window frame menu of LiteWindow.

Notice that we did not specify any of these characteristics, they were inherited from the *DefaultWindow* class. Instead of creating a canvas, decorating it with other canvases, and attaching processes listening for mouse events in the decoration canvases to perform the window operations, the program simply creates a *DefaultWindow* object with these methods precreated. And further, by replacing the implementation of *DefaultWindow* the user can supply all the windows with a consistent set of decorations.

We can replace the default window implementation by a *ScrollWindow* by changing *DefaultWindow* to be the *ScrollWindow* class object:

```
/DefaultWindow ScrollWindow store
```

Now, if we repeat our actions:

/win2   Put `win2` on the stack for later use.

framebuffer The parent of the Window is the root Window.

/new DefaultWindow send

                 Make a `new` instance of the `DefaultWindow` class.

def   Call it `win2`.

/reshapefromuser win2

send   Set size and location of `win2` from the user.

```
/map win2 send
```

Make window visible by invoking method /map.

```
/DefaultWindow LiteWindow store
```

Restore the definition of DefaultWindow.

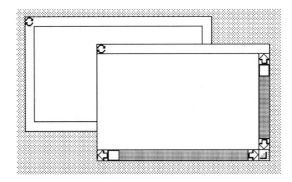

Figure: 6.7.   Creating another window after changing DefaultWindow.

This is a simple example of the power of the inheritance concept. Notice that if you now start any of the standard NeWS clients, they will look like a ScrollWindow, too.

6.3   Painting Windows

The Window object is made of several canvases, some for the frame, and one special canvas, called the client canvas, which is surrounded by the frame. It is this client canvas that the client can use to paint on.

The default window does not paint anything interesting; the canvas that is surrounded by the frame is always white. In the Lite toolkit, window objects have a method called the *PaintClient* method that is invoked whenever the image in the window needs to be painted. In order for a client to have an image painted on the blank canvas of the DefaultWindow object, it must override the object's *PaintClient* method.

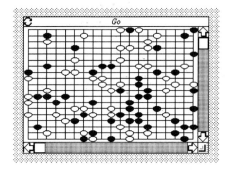

Figure: 6.8.   Running the Go demo after changing DefaultWindow.

6.3.1   The PaintClient method

We already have a suitable *PaintClient* method, the fan-of-lines procedure from Chapter 4. We can use it as our example window *win*'s *PaintClient* method, using the technique of sending an executable array to the window object. The window object already has a PaintClient method, but we can re-define it by sending the window object a procedure that does the re-defining:

```
{
    /PaintClient {
                    Re-define the PaintClient method.
        10 fanoflines
                    To be a fan of 10 lines.
    } def
} win send         In the instance win.
/PaintClient win send
                    Invoke the new PaintClient metchod.
```

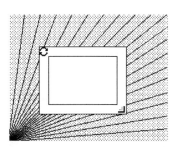

Figure: 6.9.   An error in the PaintClient method.

The result is a fan of lines in the background, and a blank window. What went wrong?

The problem is that the *fanoflines* procedure paints on the current canvas, and by default this is the root. The method was invoked without the correct context being established. Each of the window methods that NeWS developers can override, such as *PaintClient*, has a corresponding method that they are not expected to override, such as *paintclient*, which establishes the context (including making the appropriate canvas current) before invoking its opposite number.

```
/paintclient win send
```

Invoke PaintClient in the right context.

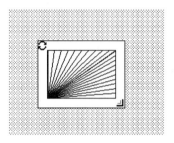

Figure: 6.10.   PaintClient method correctly invoked.

The result is a fan of lines in the window. (Notice that we were able to use a standard PostScript program as the PaintClient method for a window; often the way in which printing and displays are integrated in NeWS.)

6.3.2   When Are Windows Painted?

The fan-of-lines procedure was executed as the result of an explicit invocation of the *paintclient* method. The *paintclient* method is also invoked implicitly, by the *DefaultWindow* code itself. Grabbing the bottom-right window control and resizing the window will cause another invocation. Clicking in the top-left control to close the window, and then in the window icon to re-open it, will cause another invocation.

In general, the *paintclient* method will be invoked automatically whenever the window's client canvas is damaged (see Section 5.2.4). Client programs in NeWS must always be ready to re-paint their canvases when required.

Clients using the Lite toolkit need not take any special measures to meet this requirement, since the toolkit arranges for their *paintclient* methods to be invoked when damage repair is required.

6.3.3 The PaintIcon Method

Closing the default window reveals that it paints its window icon white just as it paints its window white. In fact, the icon is simply another canvas, like the window's client canvas, which needs a paint method. It overlaps and is overlapped by other canvases, and it too can be damaged.

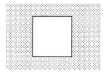

Figure: 6.11.   The default method for PaintIcon leaves a blank icon.

The icon is just another canvas; we can use the same method to paint it:

```
{
    /PaintIcon {
```
                    Define the PaintIcon method.
```
        10 fanoflines
```
                    To be a fan of 10 lines.
```
    } def
} win send
```
In the instance `win`.
```
/painticon win send
```
                    Invoke PaintIcon in correct context.

The result is a small fan of lines in the icon. Now, whenever the window is closed, the fan-of-lines procedure is run on the icon canvas, and whenever the window is opened, the same code is run on the window's canvas. This is the reason for the PaintClient vs. paintclient distinction outlined above. Notice the importance of establishing the correct context for a method that is being invoked.

Figure: 6.12.   Our PaintIcon method now shows what was happening in the window.

6.4   The Simple Lines Client

We now have a simple working NeWS client. It draws an image in its window, and in its icon. The application's window can be resized, and moved on the screen. The window overlays and is overlaid by other windows. Although the application is small enough to type into **psh** interactively, we are going to continue expanding it, and life will be easier if we keep the entire program in a file. So, here is the complete text of the "Simple Lines" client:

```
#!/usr/NeWS/bin/psh
```

> See below.

```
/fanoflines {
```

> This draws a fan of lines from 0,0 to the top and left edges. The number of lines in the fan is passed on the top of the stack.

```
gsave
```
> Preserve the graphics state.

```
0 setgray
```

> Set the current color to black.

```
matrix currentmatrix
```

> Push a copy of the current matrix onto the stack.

```
exch
```
> Exchange it with the number of lines parameter to get the number of lines onto the top of the stack.

```
clippath pathbbox
```

> Find the bounding box of the current clip path, which will be the bounding box of the window. This leaves the x and y of the lower left hand corner on the stack followed by the width and height of the window.

```
scale
```
> Scale the coordinate system by the width and height. This yields a coordinate system that ranges from 0 to 1 on both axes.

```
pop pop
```
> Ignore the lower left hand corner information, since we know it equals zero (the default).

```
newpath
```
> Clear out the current path.

```
0 1 3 -1 roll div 1 {
```

> This is a loop that steps from 0, with an increment of 1/number_of_lines (the number of lines was on the top of the stack; **roll** is used to move it around for dividing it into 1), up to 1.

```
0 0 moveto
```

```
1 1 index lineto
```

> Draw a line from (0,0) to (1,i), leaving i on the stack (i is the index variable that **for** leaves on the stack).

```
0 0 moveto 1 lineto
```

> Draw a line from (0,0) to (i,1), popping i off the stack (or rather, using it, and not making a copy to preserve it).

```
} for
```

```
0 0 moveto 1 1 lineto
```

> Draw the diagonal line.

```
setmatrix
```

> Set the coordinate system back to what it was before we scaled it (the line `matrix currentmatrix` left the current matrix on the stack).

`stroke`   Draw the lines. We have to save and restore the current matrix so that when the lines are drawn, they have the right width.

`grestore`   Restore the graphics context to the previous context. It is usually good practice for functions to leave the graphics context undisturbed.

`} def`   Finish defining the fanoflines procedure.

`/win`   Put win on the stack for later use as the name of the window.

```
framebuffer /new DefaultWindow send
```

> Send the new message, with argument framebuffer, to the default window class. This tells it to create a new instance of the class with the frame buffer as its parent.

`def`   Call the new window win.

`{`   Start creating a procedure that will be sent to the window object to set up its instance variables and override some methods.

```
/FrameLabel (Lines) def
```

> Make the FrameLabel instance variable the string "Lines" — it will be displayed in the window's frame.

```
/PaintClient { 10 fanoflines} def
```

> Make the PaintClient method of the new object be a procedure that draws a fan of 10 lines per side.

```
/PaintIcon { 10 fanoflines } def
```

Make the PaintIcon method of the new object be a
procedure that draws a fan of 10 lines per side.

`} win send`   Send the procedure to the win object to set it up.

```
/reshapefromuser win send
```

Invoke the method that interactively sizes and positions
the window.

```
/map win send
```

Invoke the method that makes the window visible.

Note that we have over-ridden one of the default window class' instance
variables by:

```
/FrameLabel (Lines) def
```

When the window is open, the frame headline will show the client's name.

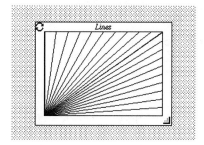

Figure: 6.13.   Results of the Simple Lines client code.

The only other change from our earlier program is the first line:
`#!/usr/NeWS/bin/psh`. For 4.2BSD-based UNIX systems, this means
that the file can be made executable and when it is executed, the remaining
lines will be given to **psh** as its standard input. In this way, NeWS can be
programmed at a command-shell level, by writing simple text files that
can be executed directly by the window system. These scripts are the major
use of **psh,** and they represent a significant difference between NeWS and
other window systems.

psh scripts mean that simple NeWS clients are truly portable:

They do not need compilation before use and are thus machine-independent.

They are ASCII files, and can be mailed or transferred through any 7-bit
medium.

They are readable, editable, and can be used as templates as the basis for
new clients.

6.5   Class Menu

After this introduction to class *Window*, we can enhance the Simple Lines
client example by using class *Menu*. Let us add a menu to set the number of
lines to be drawn, which so far has been fixed at 10:

```
#!/usr/NeWS/bin/psh
```
> Header for making the file executable.

```
/fanoflines {
```
> % Repeated from the previous example.

```
} def
/linesperside 10 def
```
> The Linesperside variable holds the number of lines per
> side that will be displayed. Initial value is 10.

```
/setlinesperside {
```
> Define a procedure that will be used to update the
> Linesperside variable.

```
  /linesperside exch store
```
> Actually do the update.

```
  /paintclient win send
```
> Since the number of lines per side changed, the image in the
> window is now out of date. We invoke the paintclient
> method to refresh it.

```
} def
```
> Finish the definition for setlinesperside.

```
/win
```
> Put win on the stack for later use as the name of
> the window.

```
framebuffer /new DefaultWindow send
```
> Send the *new* message, with argument framebuffer, to the
> default window class. This tells it to create a new instance
> of the class with the frame buffer as its parent.

```
def
```
> Call the new window win.

```
{
```
> Start creating a setup procedure for win.

134

```
/FrameLabel (Lines) def
```

> Make the FrameLabel instance variable the string "Lines"
> — it will be displayed in the window's frame.

```
/PaintClient {

  gsave clippath 1 setgray fill grestore

  linesperside fanoflines
```

`} def` Make the PaintClient method of the new object be a
procedure that clears the window and draws a fan of
the appropriate lines per side.

```
/PaintIcon { 10 fanoflines } def
```

> Make the PaintIcon method of the new object be a
> procedure that draws a fan of 10 lines per side.

```
/ClientMenu
```

> We will create a new menu object and store it into the
> ClientMenu instance variable.

```
[ (10) (20) (100) (500) ]
```

> When creating a menu object, the arguments are two
> arrays. The first array contains the strings to be displayed
> in the menu.

```
[ { currentkey cvi setlinesperside } ]
```

> The second argument is an array of the procedures to call
> when the corresponding string is selected. If the procedure
> are all the same, the array can have only a single entry.
> This procedure finds the string that was selected, converts
> it into an integer, and calls the procedure that updates the
> Linesperside variable.

```
/new DefaultMenu send dcf
```

> Send the new message to the DefaultMenu class. It will
> create a new menu object, which we will set into the
> ClientMenu instance variable.

`} win send` Send the procedure to the win object to set it up.

```
/reshapefromuser win send
```

> Invoke the method that interactively sizes and positions
> the window.

```
/map win send
```

> Invoke the method that makes the window visible.

Now, when the Simple Lines client is executed, the window is created with 10 lines per side. Displaying the menu allows the user to select a new number of lines, and when the menu disappears the window is re-painted with the new number of lines. The repainting happens because the Menu object invokes the *setlinesperside* procedure, and it in turn invokes the *paint-client* method of *win*.

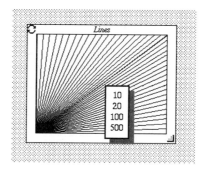

Figure: 6.14.   The Simple Lines client executing with parameters from the ClientMenu.

6.5.1   Scheduling window system activities

Notice that if you select 500 lines per side, it takes some time to finish painting the window. Try pressing the menu button during this repaint, and you will notice that the menu appears only after the repaint is complete. Delays like these are not satisfactory. They can be eliminated by adding a **pause** statement to the fan-of-lines procedure:

```
/fanoflines {
```

        This draws a fan of lines from 0,0 to the top and left edges. The number of lines in the fan is passed on the top of the stack.

    `gsave`   Preserve the graphics state.

  `0 setgray`

        Set the current color to black.

  `matrix currentmatrix`

        Push a copy of the current matrix onto the stack.

    `exch`   Exchange it with the number of lines parameter to get the number of lines onto the top of the stack.

136

```
clippath pathbbox
```

Find the bounding box of the current clip path, which will be the bounding box of the window. This leaves the x and y of the lower left hand corner on the stack followed by the width and height of the window.

```
scale
```
Scale the coordinate system by the width and height. This yields a coordinate system that ranges from 0 to 1 on both axes.

```
pop pop
```
Ignore the lower left hand corner information, since we know it equals zero (the default).

```
newpath
```
Clear out the current path.

```
0 1 3 -1 roll div 1 {
```

This is a loop that steps from 0, with an increment of 1/number_of_lines (the number of lines was on the top of the stack; **roll** is used to move it around for dividing it into 1), up to 1.

```
0 0 moveto
```

```
1 1 index lineto
```

Draw a line from (0,0) to (1,i), leaving i on the stack (i is the index variable that **for** leaves on the stack).

```
0 0 moveto 1 lineto
```

Draw a line from (0,0) to (i,1), popping i off the stack (or rather, using it, and not making a copy to preserve it).

```
pause
```
After drawing each pair of lines, we pause to allow other processes to run.

```
} for
```

```
0 0 moveto 1 1 lineto
```

Draw the diagonal line.

```
setmatrix
```

Set the coordinate system back to what it was before we scaled it (the line `matrix currentmatrix` left the current matrix on the stack).

```
stroke
```
Draw the lines. We have to save and restore the current matrix so that when the lines are the right width when they are drawn.

```
grestore
```
Restore the graphics context to its previous value.

```
} def
```
Finish defining the fanoflines procedure.

Why did the delay happen? Why did the **pause** statement cure it? When the default window object decides that the *paintclient* method should be executed, it creates (**fork**s) a new lightweight process to run it. Unlike UNIX processes, the NeWS lightweight processes are scheduled non-pre-emptively. The delay in displaying the menu was because the fan-of-lines procedure had not finished running. The **pause** statement allows other processes to run, in this case allowing the menu code to pop-up the menu.

As we explained in Chapter 5, lightweight processes are very cheap, and can be used liberally. The *Menu* class implementation, for example, forks a new lightweight process every time a menu is popped-up. This allows other activities to take place while the user is manipulating the menu. The *Window* class implementation forks a new lightweight process every time a canvas is to be repainted. In this way the repaint can be aborted (by killing the repaint process) if it is no longer useful.

Now that the Lines program no longer blocks other processes, you can see the abort of the repaint in action. Select 500 lines per side and, while it is painting, grab the bottom right corner and resize the window. As soon as you let up on the mouse button, the painting will stop, and restart at the new size. The process painting at the first size was killed, and another was created which painted at the new size.

6.6   Class Item

When the Lines client created its window, it had to supply an argument (*framebuffer*) to the **new** method of *DefaultWindow*:

```
/win framebuffer /new DefaultWindow send def
```

This argument (*framebuffer*) supplied the parent canvas for the canvas that formed the window. All canvases form part of a hierarchy whose root is the canvas representing the whole display, the *root canvas*. This hierarchy is used both for output, to restrict drawing to the boundaries of multiple overlapping drawing surfaces, and for input, to route events to the canvas containing the mouse.

6.6.1   Output and the Canvas Hierarchy

Canvases can be moved in *x* and *y* directions and repositioned "vertically" so that they either obscure or are obscured by their siblings. They can be either opaque, or transparent. Transparent canvases do not obscure images drawn beneath them by parents or siblings, and anything drawn in a transparent canvas is drawn in its parent. Canvases are cheap, and can be used liberally to divide up drawing surfaces into convenient pieces. Their shape is determined by a PostScript *path*, so that they can be any shape desired.

6.6.2 Using Canvases

We now demonstrate the use of canvases by adding another way to control the number of lines in the example, a slider control that can be manipulated by the user.

For simplicity, we change the Simple Lines client in two stages. First, the fan-of-lines procedure is given a separate canvas, a child of *Client-Canvas*, to draw in. Second, the shape of the child canvas changes to cover only part of the *ClientCanvas*, and create a *SliderItem* (which is in itself a canvas) to cover the rest.

So far in this chapter, we have been using pre-defined classes. Now, we want to define a new subclass. We turn the Simple Lines client program into the definition of a new class, LinesWindow, and extend it with a child canvas of the client canvas. This first stage involves the following steps:

creating a special *LinesWindow* subclass of the *DefaultWindow* class.

overriding the operations that create and shape the *ClientCanvas* to create and shape the child canvas too.

changing the *PaintClient* procedure to paint in the child canvas.

6.6.3 Defining the LinesWindow Subclass

To define a subclass of an existing class, NeWS provides the **classbegin** and **classend** operators:

class dict **classbegin** —

> Start defining a subclass of *class*. The *dict* holds the instance variables needed by objects in the new subclass.

— **classend** *obj*

> Finish the new subclass definition started by *classbegin*, and return *obj*, an object representing the new class.

Now, we use these operators to convert the Simple Lines client to define its window as a subclass of the DefaultWindow class:

```
#!/usr/NeWS/bin/psh

/fanoflines {

    %  Repeated from the previous example.

} def
```

```
/LinesWindow
```
> Put LinesWindow on the stack for the eventual def.
```
DefaultWindow
```
> We will make LinesWindow a subclass of DefaultWindow.
```
1 dict dup begin
```
> Create a dict big enough to hold the instance variables for the class object. Leave it on the stack, and open it.
```
  /linesperside 10 def
```
> This instance variable holds the number of lines.
```
end
```
```
classbegin
```
Start defining a new subclass of DefaultWindow.
```
  /FrameLabel (Lines) def
```
> Override the default FrameLabel variable.
```
  /PaintIcon { 10 fanoflines } def
```
> Override the default PaintIcon method.
```
  /PaintClient {
```
> Override the default PaintClient method.
```
    gsave clippath 1 setgray fill grestore
```
> Clear the window.
```
    linesperside fanoflines
```
> Draw the fan of lines.
```
  } def
  /setlinesperside {
```
> Create a method to update the number of lines per side.
```
    /linesperside exch store
```
> Update the instance variable.
```
    /paintclient self send
```
> Repaint the window. Note the use of **self**.
```
  } def
  /ClientMenu
```
> Override the default ClientMenu variable.
```
  [ (10) (20) (100) (500) ]
```

```
    [ { currentkey cvi /setlinesperside win send } ]
    /new DefaultMenu send def
classend def
```

Finish defining the new class and call it LinesWindow.

```
/win framebuffer /new LinesWindow send def
```

Create a LinesWindow object, and call it win.

```
/reshapefromuser win send
/map win send
```

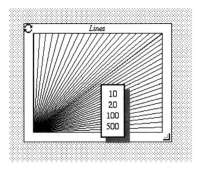

Figure: 6.15.   The new Simple Lines client works just like the old one.

This version of the Simple Lines client works just like the previous one, but the structure is simpler and the newly defined class can be re-used.

6.6.4   Adding a Canvas to LinesWindow

Now that we have re-structured the Simple Lines client to use the LinesWindow class, we can change the definition of this new class to allow the PaintClient method to draw in a child of the client canvas. To demonstrate this better, we make the child canvas round:

```
/LinesWindow
```

Put LinesWindow on the stack for later use.

```
DefaultWindow 2 dict dup begin
```

These are the class' instance variables.

```
    /linesperside 10 def
```

The number of lines per side.

```
    /LinesCanvas null def
```

A child of the ClientCanvas that we will draw in.

```
end

classbegin

    ...

    /PaintClient {

        LinesCanvas setcanvas
```

Make the class' child canvas current, and then repeat our previous actions.

```
        gsave clippath 1 setgray fill grestore

        linesperside fanoflines

    } def

    /CreateClientCanvas {
```

Override the default method that creates the client canvas.

```
        /CreateClientCanvas super send
```

Our version does whatever the DefaultWindow class does, and then ....

```
        /LinesCanvas ClientCanvas newcanvas store
```

Creates a child of the DefaultWindow class' ClientCanvas, and calls it LinesCanvas.

```
        LinesCanvas /Mapped true put
```

Map it, so that when its parent is mapped, it will become visible too.

```
    } def

    /ShapeClientCanvas {
```

We also override the ShapeClientCanvas method of the DefaultWindow class with our own version, which starts here.

```
        /ShapeClientCanvas super send
```

Our version does whatever the DefaultWindow class does, and then ....

`gsave` Save the graphics state to be on the safe side.

```
        ClientCanvas setcanvas
```

Make the DefaultWindow's ClientCanvas current.

```
        clippath pathbbox scale pop pop newpath
```

> Make the coordinates [0,0] to [1,1].

```
0.5 0.5 0.35 0 360 arc
```

> Make a circular path in the center of the canvas.

```
LinesCanvas reshapecanvas
```

> Make the LinesCanvas this circular shape.

```
grestore
```

> Restore the graphics state.

```
    } def
classend def
```

When the LinesWindow is created, it creates a round child of the default window's client canvas and maps it. Then, when the PaintClient method is invoked, it draws in this round canvas.

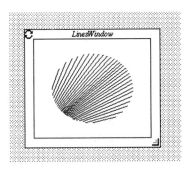

Figure: 6.16.   This Simple Lines client paints in a ''round'' child canvas.

6.6.5   Using the LiteItem Class

For the second stage, we change the *LinesWindow* class to add in a slider, change the *setlinesfromuser* procedure to update the slider, and change the *PaintClient* method to paint the slider as well:

```
#!/usr/NeWS/bin/psh
systemdict /Item known not {
    (NeWS/liteitem.ps) run
} if
```

> Load the LiteItem files if they have not already been loaded.

```
/fanoflines {
```

```
    ...
} def
/LinesWindow
DefaultWindow 3 dict dup begin
```
    ...   The other instance variables are unchanged.
```
    /LinesItem null def
```
              This one holds the slider object.
```
end
classbegin
    ...
    /PaintClient {
```
        ...   The PaintClient method is the same, except ...
```
        /paint LinesItem send
```
                that we send a /paint message to the slider so that it
                paints too.
```
    } def
    /CreateClientCanvas {
```
        ...   We now place on the stack the arguments we need to
                create a slider .
```
        /LinesItem
```
                Once we have created it, we will call it LinesItem.
```
        (Lines:)
```
                The slider has a text label, in this case `Lines:`
```
        [1 500 linesperside]
```
                This array holds the minimum, maximum, and current
                values of the slider item.
```
        /Right
```
                The slider goes to the right of its label.
```
        { ItemValue /setlinesperside win send }
```
                This proc gets invoked when the slider is activated. It
                updates the number of lines per side.
```
        ClientCanvas
```
                The slider canvas will be a child of this canvas.

144

```
/new SliderItem send store
```

Create a new object in the SliderItem class and call it
LinesItem.

```
[LinesItem] forkitems pop
```

Now fork a process controlling the slider.

```
} def
/ShapeClientCanvas {
```

..... The ShapeClientCanvas method is the same, except

```
0 0 1 0.25 /reshape LinesItem send
```

that we reshape the slider to occupy the bottom quarter of
the window.

```
grestore
} def
/setlinesperside {
```

Create a method to update the number of lines per side.

```
/linesperside exch store
```

Update the instance variable.

```
linesperside /setvalue LinesItem send
```

Update the value of the slider, so that it always reflects
the latest value even if it was set with the menu.

```
/paintclient self send
```

Repaint the window. Note the use of **self**.

```
} def
```

..... The rest of the client is unchanged.

The result is a window with a fan of lines and a slider. Drag the slider
with the left mouse button and when you let go, the fan will be repainted
with the new number of lines. Select a number from the menu, and both the
fan and the slider will be updated. Because the fan and the slider draw in
their own canvases and take their sizing parameters from the shape of these
canvases, neither the slider nor the fan code needed to be changed to allow
them to coexist in a window.

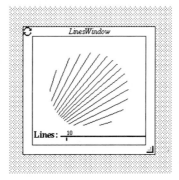

Figure: 6.17.   Now there is a slider to control the number of lines per side.

Notice again the use of lightweight processes for concurrency. You can drag the slider or pop the menus while the fan is being painted, because both the menus and the slider are managed by separate processes.

6.6.6   Input and the Canvas Hierarchy

The canvas hierarchy is not merely useful for controlling output. It also allows for control and routing of input. Note the following points:

The right button in the frame pops-up the window management menu.

The right button in the fan or the slider pops-up the number menu.

The middle button anywhere in the window drags the window around.

The left button in the frame or the fan pops the window to the front.

The left button in the slider drags the sliding cursor.

This behavior is the result of the different canvases expressing different interests in events. The slider canvas is interested only in left button events. The *LinesCanvas* is not interested in any events. So, except in the slider which intercepts left button events, all events fall through to the *ClientCanvas*. Here, the menu code has expressed interest in right button events, but others fall through to the *FrameCanvas*, which is interested in all three buttons.

146

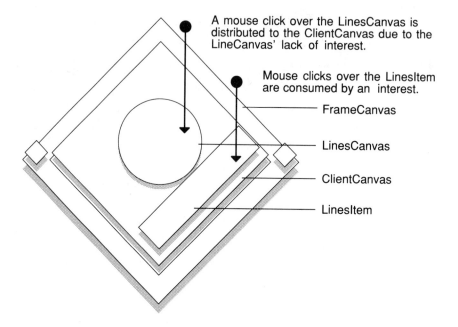

Figure: 6.18. Canvas hierarchy and event flow in the LinesWindow.

6.7 External Clients

We have shown how to use the classes that NeWS provides to create simple client programs, and how to use them as the basis for new, application-specific sub-classes. Many NeWS users have done so, creating radically different user interfaces for windows and menus that work even with pre-existing clients. For example, one prominent NeWS developer, Don Hopkins of the University of Maryland, was able to replace the menus with round, ''pie'' menus. [HOPK88, HOPK89]

All the clients we have constructed so far run entirely within the server; they are written entirely in PostScript. While this is a quick and effective way of creating simple applications, most people will want to use other programming languages. In the next chapter, we show how to use C and other languages to write programs that can exploit both PostScript programs and the class mechanism in the NeWS server.

7
NeWS Applications and the Network

"The other Messenger's called Hatta. I must have two *you know —
to come and go. One to come, and one to go."*

Lewis Carroll,
Through the Looking Glass

Up to this point we have talked about the NeWS server and about writing PostScript programs that execute in the server. However, NeWS is a *network-based* window system. Network-based window servers allow the clients to make use of window system and display resources on the network, much as a distributed file system such as NFS allows programs to make use of file system and disk resources over the network. End-users or NeWS clients can connect to remote NeWS servers to display output inside a window on the screen or receive input from the keyboard mouse or other input device.

This chapter explains how to write applications outside the server that communicate with it over a local or remote communication path. PostScript programs flow over this path from the client to the server. The protocol used by the PostScript program to reply to the client is specified by the application according to its needs.

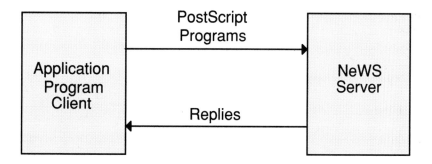

Figure: 7.1.   NeWS protocol over a network connection.

The client-server dialogue consists of four parts:

1   Establishing a connection to the server.

2   Sending PostScript code (downloading) to the server.

3   Invoking the PostScript code downloaded.

4   Sending replies from the server back to the client.

This chapter concentrates on communicating with NeWS from clients written in C.

7.1   Establishing a Connection

NeWS specifies the server to be used by client applications through the *NEWSSERVER* environment variable; by default they access the local host. The utility program **setnewshost** outputs the correct setting of the *NEWSSERVER* variable for a given remote host. A *NEWSSERVER* variable on a 4.2 BSD UNIX system may have a value something like: *3227656822.2000;paper*. The first number is the IP (Internet Protocol) address of the server in host byte order. The second number is the host's IP port number. In order to access NeWS, the application needs to create a byte stream connection, and connect it to the remote host's IP address and port. In this instance, the text name of the host upon which the server is running follows the semicolon. **setnewshost** will be implemented differently on different operating systems. For example, it may be implemented as an iconic application on a Macintosh instead of as a UNIX shell command.

In normal use, only the NeWS server and the NeWS application support library are concerned with *NEWSSERVER*. When NeWS starts up, it calculates the correct value of *NEWSSERVER* and passes it on to any applications initiated. The C client procedure call *ps_open_PostScript()* opens a connection to the NeWS server that is identified by *NEWSSERVER*. The procedure *ps_close_PostScript()* closes the connection.

The rough skeleton of a NeWS application is:

```
main(argc, argv) {
```
         . . .   Setup.

                   Try to open a connection to the NeWS server.

```
    if (ps_open_PostScript() == 0) {
```
                   Connection attempt failed.

```
        fprintf(stderr, "Could not connect to NeWS
            server.\n");
```

```
            exit(1);

    }
```

Successfully connected to server.

...   The body of the application.

The application has completed: close the connection to
the server.

```
    ps_close_PostScript();

}
```

7.2   Sending PostScript Programs to the Server

Unlike most window systems, NeWS does not currently offer a C subroutine library. The C interface is not specifically defined. Instead of having
a particular interface and subroutine library, NeWS provides a preprocessing
tool and support routines that allow interfaces to be easily constructed on a
per-client basis. Fixed interfaces to C and other languages, such as Fortran,
Lisp, and C++, are provided by a variety of user interface toolkits which
exist or are being developed for NeWS.

The preprocessor *cps* compiles a specification file into an interface. The
specification file contains C function declarations and bodies for each of
these written in the PostScript language. The interface that *cps* generates
contains the declared functions. If one of the *cps*-generated functions is
called by a client, the PostScript code in the body of the function is executed by the NeWS server.

For example, taking a look at a simple *cps* definition file:

```
cdef ps_moveto(x, y)
            x y moveto
```

The first line starts the C definition (**cdef**) of a function called
ps_moveto that takes two integer arguments: *x* and *y*. The second line is the
PostScript code that will be executed when *ps_moveto* is called. This Post-
Script code fragment that refers to the C function parameters will be
substituted into the PostScript body. In a client's C program, *ps_moveto*
can be called like any other C function:

```
ps_moveto(37,290);
```

This particular **ps_moveto** call transmits the PostScript code fragment:

```
37 290 moveto
```

to the NeWS server, where it is executed.

cps supports several types of parameters to PostScript code fragments:

int　　　　　Used for C *int*s, *long*s and *char*s. This is the default type.

float　　　　Used for C *float*s and *double*s.

string and *cstring*
　　　　　　　Used for C strings that are either null terminated (*string*) or
　　　　　　　have a count of the number of bytes in them (*cstring*). Counted
　　　　　　　strings appear as two parameters in the C function's parameter
　　　　　　　list: the pointer to the string and the count.

fixed　　　　A fixed point number represented as an integer with 16 bits
　　　　　　　after the decimal point.

token　　　　A special user defined token. This is a tool that can be used for
　　　　　　　fast access to objects in the server — it is used for performance
　　　　　　　improvement only.

The following function specifications are slightly more complex:

```
cdef ps_drawstring(x, y, string s)

        x y moveto s show

cdef ps_drawcstring(x, y, cstring s)

        x y moveto s show
```

The only difference between these two functions is that the first takes a null terminated string, the second a counted string. These functions would be used to display a string at a specific location:

```
ps_drawstring(37, 95, "Hello World");
ps_drawcstring(37, 95, "Hello World", 11);
```

Both functions transmit the same PostScript fragment:

```
        37 95 moveto (Hello World) show
```

It is important to point out, since most people are concerned with efficiency, that the ASCII form of the PostScript fragment is not generally transmitted to the server. Rather, a precompiled compressed binary form is sent instead (This will be discussed at the end of the chapter).

This model essentially comprises *cps* communications with NeWS. This simple structure enables extremely powerful tasks. For example, functions can be defined:

```
cdef defsmile()
```
```
 /smile {      % w h x y smile => -
```
Draw a smiling face.
```
    gsave
```
In the rectangle (x,y) to (x+w,y+h).
```
    translate
```
Coordinate system centered at x, y.
```
    scale
```
Coordinate system is the unit square.
```
   .5 .5 .5 0 360 arc stroke
```
Face.
```
   .5 .5 .3 225 315 arc stroke
```
Smile.
```
   .7 .7 .03 0 360 arc stroke
```
Right eye.

```
   .3 .7 .03 0 360 arc stroke
```
Left eye.
```
   .5 .5 .03 0 360 arc stroke
```
Nose.
```
    grestore
```
```
 } def
```
Define the smile function.
```
cdef smile(x, y, w, h)
```
```
   w h x y smile
```
Call the smile function.

   This code fragment defines two C functions: *defsmile* defines a PostScript function call *smile*; and *smile* (in C) calls *smile* (in PostScript). *defsmile* needs to be called only once. Each time the client wants to draw a smile, *smile* is called, avoiding the need to send the description of the image.

   Procedure definitions can be used in an open-ended way as display lists:

```
cdef ps_begindef()
```

```
/displaylist {
```
>   Start defining a function.

```
cdef ps_enddef()
```
>   } def   Close code body and define the function.

```
cdef ps_drawdisplaylist()
```
```
    displaylist
```
>   Invoke the display list function.

```
cdef ps_moveto(x, y)x y moveto
```
```
cdef ps_lineto(x, y)x y lineto
```
```
cdef ps_closepath()closepath
```
```
cdef ps_stroke()stroke
```

These definitions can be used to open and close the definition of a display list and to invoke the display list. Such functions are useful in C programs like the fragment that follows:

```
ps_begindef();
```
```
ps_moveto(100,100);
```
>   The PostScript code generated by this call won't be
>   executed directly, rather it will be added to the code
>   fragment.

```
ps_lineto(100,200);
```
```
ps_lineto(200,200);
```
```
ps_closepath();
```
```
ps_stroke();
```
```
ps_enddef();
```
>   Close off the display list definition.

```
ps_drawdisplaylist();
```
>   Execute it, causing the figure to be drawn.

How does the developer benefit from the *cps* model? NeWS and *cps* combine to allow flexible and customized C interfaces. Where reasonable, the developer can shift parts of the application into the server by using remote function definition and execution. Applications can be split into two or more pieces that run on either end of the communication link. The developer has much latitude in deciding where that split occurs.

But this flexibility itself introduces a problem. Where should the split lie? This is a common question in the design of distributed applications. Unfortunately, no hard and fast rules have emerged, but a few general principles apply:

Developers should avoid trying to keep a lot of synchronized data structures on both sides of the connection. This duplication of structure is more prone to error and can be a source of inefficiencies. Data structures should be on either the client side or the server side, and should not straddle the boundary. However, it seems acceptable to have structures on one side reference structures on the other.

Complicated data structures and computation are generally best handled on the client side. C will often outperform PostScript, since compiled languages usually outperform interpreted languages.

Operations tightly tied to user interaction, such as dragging lines or animating the change of a switch, are best done in the NeWS server because the server is closer to the display and the user.

7.3   Server to Client Communication

Above, we discussed communication from the client to the server. It is time to look at the other direction: server to client. At one level there is little to describe: the server-client protocol is determined by the client application. Since the code in the server is generated by the client, the client can strictly specify the amount and kind of information it wishes sent back from the server. The only protocol is that defined by the client. The code in the server can use the standard PostScript output primitives (such as **print**, **write**, **writestring**) to send an arbitrary sequence of bytes down the communication channel to the client.

Once again, *cps*, with a little help from the server, provides a facility for making this easier. The stream from the server to the client is made up of packets of data beginning with a *tag* that contain *typed* data. The tags form the boundaries between the packets. There are functions in NeWS to send packets and features in *cps* for receiving them.

Two kinds of client-to-server messages exist: synchronous and asynchronous. When using a synchronous message, the client sends a request to the server and then waits for a reply — the server and client are synchronized. An asynchronous message permits the server to send a message to the client without a direct request to do so.

The syntax of **cdef** in *cps* is somewhat more complicated than the functions defined so far. **cdef**'s structure is:

```
cdef cname ( arguments ) => tag ( return_values )
    PostScript_code_fragment
```

The tag and the return values are new. These values define the layout of the packet that is expected by the client in response to the execution of the code fragment. Note that the return values must appear in the argument list, and when the function is called, pointers must be provided. The tag is simply a unique integer ($-32768 \leq \text{tag} \leq 32767$).

NeWS has two operators that can be used on the server side to construct packets:

n **tagprint** —

   Starts a packet whose tag is *n*.

obj **typedprint** —

   Adds *obj* to the end of the packet.

This would be an example of a synchronous request that returns the value of a PostScript variable to the client:

```
#define GETVAR_TAG 37
```

   Use a symbolic definition for the tag.

```
cdef ps_getvar(x) => GETVAR_TAG (x)
         GETVAR_TAG tagprint
         var typedprint
```

When *ps_getvar(&q)* is invoked in the C program, it causes the following sequence of events:

The code fragment `37 tagprint var typedprint` is sent to the server.

The C program blocks, waiting for a packet with the tag *37*.

The server executes the code fragment, which transmits a packet with the tag *37* that contains one data value: the value of the variable *var*.

The C program receives the tag and data and stores it in *q*.

An asynchronous *cps* definition omits the PostScript code fragment:

```
#define MENUHIT_TAG 38
  cdef ps_menuhit(index) => MENUHIT_TAG (index)
```

The function *ps_menuhit* tests to see if the first packet in the clients input queue is tagged with *MENUHIT_TAG*. If it is, the packet is read and stored into the return value, index, and the function returns true; otherwise, the function returns false and does not change the input queue. If the input queue is empty, the client waits until it is not.

These tagged packets are created in the server by calling **tagprint** and **typedprint** in the usual way, except that the calls are usually done in response to some external event that was not triggered directly by the client. The function used in this example could be used to receive messages from a menu package: when the user makes a selection, the PostScript code sends a *MENUHIT* packet back to the client.

Asynchronous definitions are typically used in the heart of the client's command interpretation loop by cascading them in a polling fashion. Extending the chapter's first example that gave the skeleton of an application, we add the body of the application:

```
main(argc, argv) {
    ...         Setup.
    if (ps_open_PostScript() == 0) {
        fprintf(stderr, "Could not connect to NeWS
            server.\n");
        exit(1);
    }
    ps_initialize();
                A cps function to set things up in the server.
    while (!psio_eof(PostScriptInput) &&
            !psio_error(PostScriptInput))
        if (ps_menuhit(&item)) {
        ...     Handle a menu selection.
        }
        else if(ps_damaged()) {
        ...     Handle damage repair.
        }
        else break;
    ps_close_PostScript();
}
```

7.4   cps and Compressed PostScript

Although it is not necessary to understand the inner workings of the program stubs generated by *cps* in order to write NeWS clients, understanding the internals is both interesting and instructive. The foundation of the communication between the client and the server is the reliable byte stream connection established by the client to the server.

Data is communicated between the partners through a stream of typed objects defined on top of the byte stream. A typed object is simply a byte that describes the object followed by the object itself. For example, an integer that can be represented in 8 bits can be transmitted in two bytes: 0200, followed by a byte containing the integer. For a full description of the communication format, see the *"Byte Stream Format"* section of the NeWS Manual. All of these typed objects are introduced by a byte whose top bit is one, i.e. the byte is 128. If the top bit is zero, then it is a normal ASCII character.

When *cps* compiles a PostScript code fragment it translates the sequence of tokens into a sequence of bytes that are ready to be transmitted to the NeWS server. There are three classes of tokens in the code fragments.

Compressed binary token This would represent a type such as a number, a
   string or a well-known built-in primitive (like **moveto**).
   Cps substitutes the binary representation for the token.

Formal parameter reference *cps* inserts a place holder which the runtime
   routine will replace with a compressed binary token that contains the
   value of the actual parameter.

ASCII keywords This class is really limited to keywords outside the other
   two classes that *cps* does not understand. These keywords are left alone
   in their original ASCII form.

The client runtime routine merely takes the array of bytes, performs the parameter substitution, and transmits it to the server. It looks remarkably like a version of the C *printf* function: the first parameter is a pointer to the server connection block, the second is a string that contains markers indicating where values should be substituted, and the rest are the values that get substituted. The result is that the client side runtime support for NeWS is very simple and small.

7.5   A Graph Example

This sample program illustrates the way in which a C client would use **cdef** to define PostScript functions inside the server. It uses one main *cps* definition, *ps_initialize*, to set things up by creating a window with an attached menu. The menu sends an asynchronous message back to the client telling which item in the menu was selected.

The program displays the graph of one of four functions in the window. The C program initializes its window and then goes into a loop waiting for menu selections. The menu is used to select one of four functions. Whenever a new function is selected, the C program redefines the display list and asks for it to be redrawn:

```
% cps header file for the function display program
#define MENUHIT_TAG 1
cdef ps_initialize()
    /displaylist {} def
```
            Define an empty display list.
```
    /paintchart {
```
            A function to paint the chart.
```
    gsave
    win /ClientCanvas get setcanvas
    clippath pathbbox
```
            Get the window width and height.
```
    3 div
```
            Height divided by 3.
```
    exch 13 div exch
```
            Width divided by 13.
```
    scale  new coordinate system is 13x3
    pop pop
```
            Erase the other two values left by pathbbox.
```
    erasepage
    0 1.5 translate
```
            Put 0,0 in the middle at the left.
```
    0 0 moveto 13 0 lineto
    stroke
```
            X axis.
```
    0 0 moveto
```

```
        displaylist
```
> Invoke the display list function.
```
        stroke
```
> Draw it.
```
        grestore
    } def
```
> Create a window.
```
/win framebuffer /new DefaultWindow send def
    {
```
> Install application-specific handlers in the window
> instance.

> The label that goes at the top of the window frame:
```
        /FrameLabel (Function Chart) def
```
> The procedure that gets called when the client part of the
> window needs to be repainted:
```
        /PaintClient {paintchart} def
```
> The menu associated with the client part of the window:
```
        /ClientMenu
          [(sin) (cos) (damped) (sum)]
          [ { MENUHIT_TAG tagprint
              /currentindex self send
              typedprint } ]
          /new DefaultMenu send def
    } win send
```
> Shape the window.
```
/reshapefromuser win send
```
> Activate the window.
```
/map win send
```
> Map the window - damage causes PaintClient to be called.
```
cdef ps_begincurve()
```
> Begin redefining the display list.
```
    /displaylist {
```

```
cdef ps_endcurve()
```

Finish the redefinition of the display list.

```
    } def paintchart
```

After the curve has been defined, paint it.

```
cdef ps_menuhit(index) => MENUHIT_TAG (index)
cdef ps_lineto(float x, float y) x y lineto
```

Here is the C program that uses these definitions:

```
#include <stdio.h>
#include <math.h>
#include "func.h"
```

Include the definitions generated from the *cps* specification.

```
main() {
    int index;
    float x, y;
```

Connect to the NeWS server:

```
    if (ps_open_PostScript() == 0) {
        fprintf(stderr, "Can't contact NeWS server\n");
        exit(1);
    }
```

Create the window.

```
    ps_initialize();
```

Loop waiting for input events:

```
    while (!psio_eof(PostScriptInput) &&
            !psio_error(PostScriptInput))
        if (ps_menuhit(&index)) {
            ps_begincurve();
```

Start redefining the display list.

```
            for (x = 0; x<=13; x += .1) {
                switch(index) {
```

Execute the appropriate function.

```
                case 0:y = sin(x);break;
```

```
        case 1:y = cos(x);break;
        case 2:y = sin(x)*exp(-x/3)*3;
        break;
        case 3:y = sin(x) + .1*sin(x*5+1);
        break;
        default: y = 0;
        }
        ps_lineto(x, y);
```

Add a point to the display list.

```
    }
    ps_endcurve();
```

Finish off the display list.

```
  } else break;
```

Terminate when the connection closes.

```
  ps_close_PostScript();
}
```

Figure 7.2 shows the window that would be created when the program is run. The borders and decorations around the edges are drawn by the Default-Window class. The curve that is drawn was chosen by selecting "damped" from the menu, which you see popped up over the window with the cursor pointing at "damped".

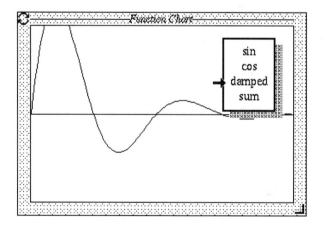

Figure: 7.2.   Function Graph program being run.

7.6   Conclusion

NeWS can be programmed at three different levels, two of which this book discusses. At the lowest level, the programmer deals with an entirely PostScript world, writing programs that are downloaded into the server. The programmer typing simple exploratory programs directly to the server, as described in Chapter 4, works at this level, as does the author of a complex window system package using multiple light-weight processes, such as a window manager or a menu package, discussed in Chapters 5 and 6.

This chapter has described the next level, where the programmer is building a bridge between the PostScript world of the server and the more familiar C world of the application. The programmer is defining either application-specific procedures or the primitives found in another window-system interface, for the purposes of emulating that interface. Programmers write a specification file which associates C procedure names with Post-Script code that is to be sent to the server when the C procedure is invoked by the client. This specification is compiled by *cps* into a C header file that is included by C application programs.

At the highest level, the programmer works in an entirely C world. The existence of PostScript is completely hidden. The programmer makes use of procedures which have been defined using the *cps* mechanism, in the same way as he would use any other C function. This level is addressed by higher-level toolkits which would be placed on top of NeWS and the Lite toolkit, and is not explicitly discussed in this book.

The next chapter examines a single NeWS application in some detail, focussing on the decisions a programmer needs to make about which of these levels is appropriate for the task at hand.

8
A Tour Through a NeWS Application

"All craftsmen share a knowledge. They have held
Reality down fluttering to a bench."

Victoria Sackville-West

This chapter reviews a relatively large NeWS application and explains some of the ways that it uses NeWS to advantage. The application is *ched*, a *ch*eap *ed*itor built as a demonstration of how to build a WYSIWYG editor in NeWS. The source for this application is in the public domain and available from Sun Microsystems. The last section in this chapter explains how to obtain the *ched* program.

Ched is a fairly simple WYSIWYG (what you see is what you get) editor. It implements automatic line breaking, left- and right- margin justification, and selections using the mouse. In Figure 8.1 is a set of snapshots of *ched* being run, along with a commentary on what is happening at each step.

This chapter begins with a section on the general structure of *ched*. This segment is followed by a series of sections on various key points in the implementation of *ched* that are relevant to its use of NeWS. The points to be covered are:

Fixed point arithmetic.

How *ched* uses NeWS to display the document.

Font information.

Use of *usertokens*.

Debug initialization.

Input events with names.

Responding to damage.

Selections.

Typeahead.

Ched uses a number of real-time layout algorithms, which will not be described in detail in this chapter. Interested developers should obtain the *Ched* application in order to get more information from the source code.

8.1 ched in Action

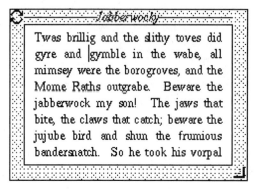

Figure: 8.1.   The ched window.

When *ched* is started it creates a window and displays the document in it. It automatically breaks lines between words to put as many words on a line as possible, without extending beyond the right margin. *Ched* enlarges the spaces between words in order to align the right edge of each line.

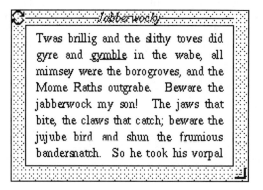

Figure: 8.2.   Selecting text.

The current position, or dot as it is referred to in some other editors, has a width in addition to a position. If the width is zero, then it is displayed as a vertical line, as in the previous screen. In this screen, an entire word, "gymble" has been selected by pressing the left mouse button between the space and the "g", and sweeping the mouse right with the button down.

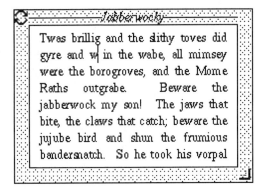

Figure: 8.3.   Replacing text.

After the word "gymble" was selected, a single "w" was typed. This caused "gymble" to be deleted and "w" inserted in its place. Notice that the document has been reformatted so that the right edges remain aligned and there are as many words as possible on each line.

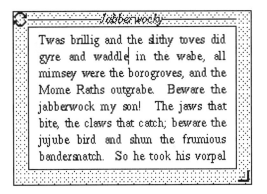

Figure: 8.4.   Continuous update of the ched window.

The rest of the word "waddle" is typed and, as it is typed, the document is continuously reformatted to look as it would if it were printed. Ched is engaged in a dialogue with NeWS, continuously receiving characters, updating internal data structures, and sending descriptions to NeWS of the reformatted image.

8.2   General Structure

Ched follows the model/view/controller paradigm that is used in Small-talk. There are two key data structures, and three key segments of the program. The first data structure is the *document*. It represents the actual text of the document being edited. It has a number of subsidiary data structures that contain the characters in the document, the formatting information, a set of markers that indicate portions of the document, and a list of the views on the document. There are a set of routines that deal with these structures. These structures and procedures form the *model* portion of *ched*. The next data structure is the *view*. It contains the actual visible representation of the document. It is what maps the document onto the screen, and hence is the part of *ched* most closely connected to NeWS. This, and its subsidiary data structures form the *view* component of the paradigm. These two are glued together by the *controller* that provides the user interface.

The Figure 8.2 shows how these parts relate to each other and to NeWS. *Ched* downloads PostScript code to NeWS that reads keystrokes and mouse events and sends these off to the controller portion of *ched*. The controller decides what to do with the character and updates the model in response. When the model is updated, information is fed back to the view to tell it that something has changed. Periodically, the view uses the updated information from the model to send PostScript graphics operators to NeWS that draw the new visible representation of the altered document.

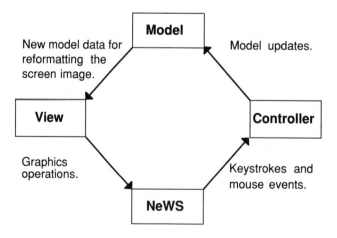

Figure: 8.5.   The flow of information amongst the various parts of ched.

8.3 Fixed Point Arithmetic

Internally, *ched* does all of its computations in units of points (approximately 1/72 of an inch). Besides being a generally convenient unit for use in documents, it is also the default unit in PostScript. But points are not sufficiently accurate for general use: a finer precision is needed. *Ched* uses fixed point numbers, with 16 bits of fractional precision, and 16 bits of integer precision, including sign. This fits in very well with most modern computer architectures that have standardized on 32 bit words. Here are the declarations necessary for dealing with these fixed point numbers:

```
typedef long fixed;
```
> 32 bit fixed point number with 16 bits of fraction.

```
#define fixedi(i)  (fixed)((i)*(1<<16))
```
> Convert int to fixed.

```
#define floorfr(fr)  ((fr)>>16)
```
> Convert fixed to int by flooring.

```
#define floatfr(f)  ((double)f/(1<<16))
```
> Convert fixed to float.

```
#define FIXED_HUGE  0x7FFFFFFF
```
> The largest possible fixed point value.

These definitions provide the basic tools for declaring fixed point numbers and converting between them, integers, and floating point numbers. One fixed point number may be added to another by using standard integer addition, and one can be multiplied or divided by an integer by using the integer operation. Unfortunately, multiplying or dividing one fixed point number by another is more complicated, but *ched* never does this.

A very significant advantage to using this form of fixed point number is that *cps* has special facilities for them. *Cps* understands the fixed declaration and can efficiently ship numbers to and from the server in this format. For example, the following declaration appears in ched.cps:

```
cdef ps_frmoveto(fixed x, fixed y) x y moveto
```

Then the call ps_frmoveto (fixedi(1)/2,fixedi(1)/2) generates the PostScript fragment 0.5 0.5 moveto. This is especially efficient since the NeWS server internally uses fixed point numbers wherever possible, to avoid floating point.

8.4   Displaying the Document

In PostScript, as in all other languages, the execution speed of a program is very closely related to how well it is written. Therefore *ched* pays quite a bit of attention to writing clean code to send to NeWS. Developers who write applications that generate PostScript, either for a printer or NeWS, are often seduced by PostScript's programmability.

In particular, there is a tendency to download procedure definitions that define a graphics model that is more familiar than the graphics model of the PostScript language. This extensive downloading of code can incur extra overhead in the NeWS server, where operations are more expensive than they are in the application. The PostScript language is, after all, an interpreted language. If, instead of substituting another model, the PostScript language graphics model is used directly for the application, the performance benefits are large. Once again, this rule holds for both NeWS and PostScript printers.

Ched uses the basic PostScript operators wherever possible, and it attempts to generate the most efficient code possible. For displaying documents, *ched* actually only generates five PostScript fragments:

x y **moveto**   Sets the current position to *x,y*.

f **setfont**   Sets the current font to *f*.

s **show**   Draws string *s*.

x 0 32 s **widthshow**

>   Draws string *s* with *x* added to the width of every space. Widthshow is used on lines that are right justified, show is used on those that are not.

w h x y **ERS**

>   Erase a rectangle starting at *x,y* whose size is *w,h*. This is the only PostScript procedure call ever generated during document display.

With these five operators, *ched* is able to do everything it needs in displaying a document. It is very careful to only invoke **setfont** if the font is really changing. It only invokes **ERS** if the rectangle really needs erasing. And it attempts to draw the longest strings possible. One easy way to sacrifice a lot of performance is to use **show** for each word, and to call **moveto** to reposition at the beginning of each word. When there is a sequence of words with equal spacing between them, it is far more efficient to call **moveto** once, and **widthshow** once. *Ched* takes advantage of the fact that it is using fixed point numbers: it can specify a width to **widthshow** that is a fractional number of pixels. NeWS will use this and distribute the error amongst the spaces between the words such that some of the spaces are one pixel wider than others. Because of this, a line of right justified text with no font or baseline changes is drawn using exactly one **moveto** and exactly one **widthshow**.

8.5   Font Information

Ched frequently needs to measure the width of strings of text. It could do this by sending the strings over to the server and asking the server to measure them, but that would incur massive message transmission penalties. Instead, it asks the server for a table of widths for each font that it's using, and uses that table locally.

First, we look at the straightforward C language declaration of the font structure used by *ched*. It contains the name of the font (e.g. *"Times-Roman"*), its point size (e.g. *12*), the height of the bounding box of all the characters, the depth of descenders from the baseline, the number of characters, an "index" for the font, and the actual array of widths. The *index* of the font is a NeWS identifier that refers to the PostScript font. The overall font structure is:

```
struct font {
  struct font *next;
```
Fonts are in a linked list.
```
  char *name;
```
Family name.
```
  char size;
```
Size in points.
```
  char bbheight;
```
Height from highest ascender to lowest descender.
```
  char descent;
```
Distance from lowest descender to baseline.
```
  unsigned short nchars,
```
The number of characters in the font.
```
  fontindex;
```
The magic token by which the server knows this font.
```
  fixed width[256];
```
The array of widths.
```
};
```

This structure is used by the C function *ft_create* that takes a font name and size and returns an associated font structure. *ft_create* first checks if that font is already known, and if so, returns the known font structure. If the font is unknown, *ft_create* sends a message to the NeWS procedure (*ps_defstr*) that requests information about the font. Once *ft_create* has got the basic information, it allocates a font structure and fills it in. *Ps_defstr* follows its return results by a stream of widths. This stream is picked up one-by-one and stuffed into the array using *ps_getint*.

```
struct font *
ft_create(name, size)
 char *name;
{
 register struct font *f;
 register index;
 int length;
 int bbheight;
 int descent;
 for (f = fontroot; f; f = f->next)
     if (f->size == size && f->name[0] == name[0]
  && f->name[1] == name[1]
         && strcmp(name, f->name) == 0)
      return f;
 index = ps_next_user_token++;
 ps_defstr(name, size, index, &length, &bbheight,
  &descent);
 f = (struct font *) malloc(sizeof(struct font) +
     (length >> 1) * sizeof f->width[0] +
  strlen(name));
 f->next = fontroot;
 fontroot = f;
 f->size = size;
 f->fontindex = index;
 f->nchars = length >> 1;
 f->name = (char *) &f->width[f->nchars];
 f->bbheight = bbheight;
 f->descent = descent < 0 ? -descent : descent;
 strcpy(f->name, name);
 for (index = f->nchars; --index >= 0;)
     ps_getint(&f->width[index]);
 return f;}
```

Ps_defstr looks up the font and scales it, and passes the scaled font and the font index, to a PostScript function called *DFS*. *DFS* returns the height, descent, and number of characters in the font.

```
#define DEFSTR_TAG 1
cdef ps_defstr(string name, size, index,
        length, bbheight, descent)
    => DEFSTR_TAG (bbheight, descent, length)
        name findfont size scalefont dup index DFS
```

When *DFS* is called, the index is on the top of the stack, and two copies
of the font lie below the index. *DFS* first executes **setfileinputtoken**
which defines the font as a user defined token, making use of the index.
(User defined tokens and how they work will be discussed in the following
section). It then sends back the information needed by *ft_create*:

```
/DFS {
 setfileinputtoken
 DEFSTR_TAG tagprint
 begin
    currentdict dup fontheight typedprint
    fontdescent typedprint
    WidthArray dup length typedprint
    aload length 2 div { pop typedprint } repeat
 end
} def
```

ps_getint is the last important function which is used by *ft_create*. It
simply receives a fixed point number from the server. It has only a return
result, with no body of PostScript code to be sent to NeWS and no tag to
wait for in return.

```
cdef ps_getint(fixed x) => (x)
```

8.6   Use of User Tokens

In the previous section on fonts, there was a small piece of magic left un-
explained that involved the **setfileinputtoken** NeWS primitive. This
primitive makes use of the NeWS user defined token facility. Chapter 7 discussed tokens briefly, and how *cps* and Compressed PostScript make use of
tokens in order to compress data for transmission. NeWS has a mechanism,
supported by *cps*, where a client program and the server can cooperatively
agree on the definition of a user token. This allows for efficient protocol
definition for a specific application. The NeWS reference manual gives more
detail about tokens and their definition, but we discuss them briefly here.

There is an array of PostScript objects associated with each input stream.
The NeWS protocol and *cps* have facilities that allow references to these

objects to be efficiently encoded in the stream that flows from the application to NeWS. These references are represented by indexes into this array. **setfileinputtoken** puts a PostScript object, in this case a font, into this array. *cps* encodes a reference to this object when the parameter type *token* is used:

```
cdef ps_do_usefont(token font) font setfont
```

The C program calls *ps_do_usefont* is called with the index that was passed to **setfileinputtoken** and stored in the font structure. The global variable *ps_next_user_token*, which is referenced in *ft_create*, simply keeps track of the next available slot in the array.

8.7   Debug Initialization

Almost all of the interface-code fragments defined in the *ched cps* specification file are quite simple. One, however, is not. It is the piece that initializes the environment in the server. It contains the definitions of procedures that create windows, define fonts, handle input events, and an assortment of other things. These definitions are is kept in a file that is separate from the *cps* specification file. In the specification file, the following lines appear:

```
cdef ps_startup()
#ifdef DEBUG
    (/home/norquay/jag/ched/ched.ps) run
#else
#include "ched.ps"
#endif
```

The initialization file is dynamically loaded from the file *ched.ps* when *ched* is being debugged. Once *ched* is stable and not being debugged, the initialization code is statically compiled into *ched*. This has the advantage when debugging that ched.ps can be altered, and the new version tested, without recompiling *ched*. Once the debugging cycle is finished, there is one less file to be bundled into the release and potentially installed incorrectly.

8.8   Input Events with Names

The input loop in *ched* is as follows:

```
#define KEYSTROKE_TAG 2
  {   clear awaitevent begin
      ClientCanvas setcanvas
```

```
    { Name type /integertype eq
        { KEYSTROKE_TAG tagprint WindowID typedprint
          Name typedprint }
        { KeyActions Name get cvx exec } ifelse
    } stopped
    end
} loop
```

Whenever an event is received, its /**Name** field is inspected. If it contains an integer, then it is just a simple keystroke, and a message containing the integer is sent to the client. Otherwise, the name is looked up in the **Key-Actions** dictionary and whatever value is found will be executed. The **KeyActions** dictionary contains a set of procedures whose names match the names of special events generated by NeWS. The *stopped* and *clear* primitives in the input loop above are used here as guards and cleanup in the case of missing *KeyActions*.

For instance, /**LeftMouseButton** is defined as a procedure that sends a message to the application saying that the left mouse button has gone up or down, depending on the /**Action** field. Besides sending the message to the application, the procedure either enables or disables the catching of /**MouseDragged** events, depending on whether the button is going down or going up. This sequence avoids the overhead of dealing with drag events when no button is pressed. Also, since this enabling happens in the NeWS server, and with the scheduling guarantees given by NeWS, the downstroke and enable happen *atomically*: there is no chance that an up event can happen in the meantime, which might be missed and cause the system to get stuck receiving drag events.

8.9   Responding to Damage

In the previous examples in this book, the execution of most graphics operations has been triggered by the invocation of the /*PaintClient* method in the window. The typical simple application defines this method as a procedure that draws the entire contents of the window. When the window gets damaged, a /**Damaged** event generated. This event is caught by a handler that invokes the /*FixFrame* method. /*FixFrame* sets the clipping to the damaged region, repaints the frame, calls /*PaintClient*, and finally resets the clipping.

ched's NeWS side doesn't have enough information for /*PaintClient* to repair the display. It needs to send a message to the client requesting the information. It would be incorrect to have /*PaintClient* send the message since it is called in the midst of the damage repair context established by /*FixFrame*. The repair cannot actually be started until the client gets the message and sends the information to handle it. Another reason that repair cannot be started yet is that requests in flight from the client to the server still have to be executed - they were generated without knowledge that a repair was needed.

ched overrides */FixFrame* with a procedure that send a message to the client side. So when damage occurs, nothing else happens immediately. In particular, the record that NeWS keeps of what region has been damaged is untouched. If more damage occurs before the application side gets around to dealing with the first damage request, the two damages will get merged and the application will see them as one.

When the client side of *ched* receives one of these messages, it replies with a message that contains a "start redraw" request, the PostScript code necessary to redraw the window, and an "end redraw" request. Start and end redraw are essentially the same as */FixFrame* broken in half: the part before */PaintClient* and the part following.

8.10   Selections

When people first see NeWS they are often seduced by the fact that they can program the server. For performance, they try to avoid client/server messages by putting as much code as possible in the server. Sometimes this is reasonable, and sometimes it is not. The decision about client/server distribution of code should be based on whether the programming environment in the server is appropriate.

ched has a quite elaborate database describing the document and its formatting properties. This database has to be accessed very rapidly using quite sophisticated algorithms. The PostScript language is not very good for this kind of processing; C is far better. So almost all of *ched* is written in C, with only a thin layer being written using PostScript code.

An example of a situation in *ched* where this trade-off between C and PostScript is hard to make is in the code that handles selections. From the users point of view, making a selection progresses through three stages:

The user positions the mouse at one end of the selection and presses down on the mouse button. The caret appears as a vertical line at the division between two characters nearest the mouse.

The user moves the mouse with the button down to extend the selection. As the mouse is being moved, the caret is echoed as a line that underlines the characters between the start of the selection and the position of the mouse.

Finally the user's finger comes off the mouse button, which defines the end
of the selection.

The middle phase is difficult because the echoing of the underline that indicates the extent of the selection depends critically on the text that is
selected: it is always at the baseline of the text and ends at the boundary
between two characters. This involves a fairly expensive calculation using
the document database. There are two choices:

send messages back and forth between the client and the server each time the
mouse moves and let the client side deal with the update,

or download enough code so that the server side can deal with it.

In *ched* the first choice was taken. This choice makes the server side of
the application quite small and puts the responsibility for efficient calculation on the client side. Performance of *ched* depends heavily on the
performance of message passing between the server and the client. In most
environments, the performance is very good, so *ched* works very well. If
ched is run at some distance from the server, with low speed communication lines or network gateways in the way, it will perform poorly. On the
other hand, a bigger investment in server-side code could have been made,
but it probably would not perform as well as the C implementation.

An alternative to what ched does is to "cheat". Often it is possible to
approximate the visual feedback entirely on the server, based on only a
limited amount of information. For example, ched could have placed in the
server an array of the y coordinates of the baselines of the text. The high-
light could follow the mouse and properly outline the text, except that the
selection would not always end exactly between two characters.

8.11 Typeahead

No computer is ever fast enough. Suppose an editor is displaying complicated real-time animation of typesetting a document. The user can probably
type faster than the editor can echo if each character is echoed when it's
received. This is the well-known typeahead problem. If implemented
properly, the model/view/controller paradigm has the advantage that the
typeahead problem disappears. The key factor is that the connection between
the model and the controller is decoupled from the connection between the
model and the view. When the model is updated, the view is not necessarily
updated. The controlling loop of *ched* looks like this:

1   While there are user keystrokes in the input queue, process them.
     These update the model only.

2   Invoke the view to update the screen according to the new state
     of the model.

3   Wait while the input queue is empty.

4   Go back to step 1.

Input events are being batched together. If the user manages to type faster than the system can echo, it will just start echoing more keystrokes at once, quickly catching up.

8.12   How to Get Ched

Ched can be obtained by sending electronic mail to *"news-archive@sun.com"* (from the ARPAnet) or *"sun!news-archive"* from usenet. The subject field of the message you send should be *"send Applications ched.shar"*. An automated mail handling program will send the source file to you by return mail. The *news-archive* is a collection of generally useful NeWS documents and sample programs. A subject line of *"help"* will return to you a description of the archive and how to get information from it.

9
Porting NeWS to Other Platforms

"There is much virtue in a window. It is to a human being as a frame is to a painting, as a proscenium to a play, as "form" to literature. It strongly defines its content."

Max Beerbohm

9.1   Introduction

''NeWS was designed to be portable.'' What exactly does this mean? It means that it should be possible, with relatively little effort, to adapt the NeWS server to run on a variety of different:

CPU architectures.

Operating systems.

Display hardware types.

Based on the authors experience of porting the Andrew and X10 window systems, the internal structure of the NeWS server was divided into three major areas, as shown in Figure 9.1 below:

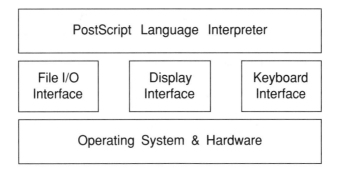

Figure: 9.1.   The NeWS server and its interfaces to its environment.

The diagram is somewhat misleading, since the vast bulk of the code is in two pieces, the interpreter and the high-performance imaging library that forms the display driver for simple framebuffers that have no graphics hardware support. All this code is written in C, and the Sun Portable Software Products team have themselves ported it to the Digital Equipment Corporation microVAX and a standard 386 PC to ensure its portability.

Despite this, faced with the source and a new piece of hardware, you can expect one or all of the three basic porting problems:

Operating systems differences. NeWS comes with operating systems interface code for both Berkeley and System V versions of UNIX, but your operating system may differ.

Display and keyboard hardware differences. NeWS comes with drivers for 1- and 8-bit memory framebuffers, but even if your hardware is of this type the details of how you get access to it will likely differ. And in many cases, your display will have graphics accelerator hardware that NeWS can use to advantage.

CPU and C compiler differences. NeWS assumes a homogeneous memory model, and the first machines it was ported to all had 32-bit integers and pointers.

To illustrate these problems in a practical context, this chapter gives case histories based on three customers' experiences. Parallax Graphics, Inc. ported NeWS to a video graphics board. Silicon Graphics, Inc. to a high-performance graphics workstation. Both of these ports illustrate the ways in which NeWS can be adapted to exploit advanced display capabilities. The Architech Corporation ported NeWS to the OS/2 operating system on IBM PC-compatible personal computers, illustrating how it can be adapted to other operating systems and CPU architectures.

The rest of this chapter is largely the work of Martin Levy from Parallax Graphics, Mark Callow from Silicon Graphics, and Maurice Balick from Architech Corporation. The NeWS Book authors are very grateful for their significant contributions, but remain responsible for any errors and omissions in these areas.

9.2   Port of NeWS to the Parallax Viper Graphics Board

In the following pages we will discuss the port of NeWS to the Viper display board from Parallax Graphics. The Viper boardset has the ability to show live video images as well as graphics data on the same screen. The display memory (1280 x 1024) is 8 bits deep, but can contain either graphics data (1 of 256 colors) or video images stored in a Pseudo-YUV[1] format.

---

1. Pseudo-YUV is a term used to describe a coding scheme for color images.
This format stores the image as lumanance and chrominance value pairs.

We present the advantages of a windowing system when it has the ability to show live video within a window on its monitor. We also describe the implementation of the server, the usage of video features within a PostScript program and finally, show an example program.

9.2.1 Server Implementation

In order to support live video, Parallax Graphics boards store display data in two different formats in display memory. A separate bitplane is used to direct video output circuitry to areas of the display that are video. These video areas must begin and end on modulus 16 horizontal (X) boundaries or unsightly gaps will appear. Video areas are represented in NeWS as canvases with a special **Video** attribute in their canvas dictionary (See Chapter 5). **Video** attributes are Boolean, and can be both set and read.

The programmer will probably never need to directly set the value of the **Video** attribute. A sub-class of the *DefaultWindow* class is defined, which overrides the map and reshape methods to enforce the modulus 16 horizontal boundary conditions and gives the various canvases that make up the window the necessary **Video** attribute. Here is the definition of this *VideoWindow* class:

```
/VideoWindow DefaultWindow
```
> Start defining a sub-class of DefaultWindow that will be called VideoWindow.

```
dictbegin dictend
```
> This dictionary will hold the instance variables.

```
classbegin
```
Start defining the methods for the new class.

```
    /map {
```
Override the map method.

```
        /map super send
```
> Do whatever DefaultWindow does for map.

```
        FrameCanvas /Video true put
```
> Then make the FrameCanvas into a Video canvas.

```
        ClientCanvas /Video true put
```
> Then make the ClientCanvas, which overlays it into a Video canvas too.

```
        IconCanvas /Video true put
```
> Finally, make the IconCanvas into a Video canvas, too.

```
    } def
```
Finish overriding the map method.

180

```
/move {      Override the move method.

    exch     With a method that restricts the location of the window
             to a multiple of 16 horizontally.

    -16 and exch

    /move super send

             Then do whatever DefaultWindow does for move.

} def

/reshape {

             Override the reshape method.

    exch 15 add -16 and

             Make sure that the width is a multiple of 16.

    exch 4 -1 roll

             Position the horizontal position in the stack.

    -16 and 4 1 roll

             Restrict that to a multiple of 16.

    /reshape super send

             Finally do DefaultWindow's reshape method.

    } def

classend def

             Finish overriding the reshape method, and then finish
             defining the VideoWindow class.
```

A **Video** canvas containing live video will obtain damage differently
than a normal NeWS canvas. Damage will be received any time the live video canvas is moved, obscured, or unobscured. Because of the large offscreen
memory size available, several video canvases can be retained without using
any host memory. The amount of offscreen memory available for canvas
cache is determined at start-up time.

Setting or resetting the **Video** boolean in the canvas "magic" dictionary
invokes C code in the device driver. It is used to set the memory on the
board into the correct mode and control overlay colors and window clipping.

Video canvases can be live. Bits on the screen will be updated from the
NTSC video input on the board without any interaction of the host processor (and hence the NeWS server). This means that if the canvas is moved,
the live video must be stopped and then restarted in the new canvas area.
Unmapping the canvas also stops the live video.

Because the Parallax video board has more than one video input, a **Present Video Input** number was added to the current graphics context. The PostScript command **vsource** will change the selected input for the present graphics context and the **initgraphics** command will reset the selected input number to zero.

The video regions on the screen have a separate colormap, hence any graphics (such as menus, buttons, and overlay graphics) need to have the color-table value computed differently. NeWS has a static colormap that allows an acceptable selection of colors to be shown on the screen. The video regions on the Parallax Graphics Board will only show 32 colors for the graphics overlays, so a subset of the normal colors are used within this area. These colors are more than enough to have most applications run without seeing much change. (For example, many of the standard demonstration programs supplied with NeWS will show quite acceptable colors when run as an overlay to a video picture).

9.2.2   NeWS Operators for Video

The following operators perform a variety of video related operations in the NeWS environment.

priority x y **vstart** —

> fills the current PostScript path with live video. *x* and *y* determines the offset of the lower left hand corner of the canvas relative to the incoming video frame. *priority* is used by the board to control the amount of time spent doing graphics or video operations.

vstop —   **vstop** stops the current live video path. If no video paths are active, no action is taken.

string **readcanvas** *canvas*

> The standard **readcanvas** operator, as defined in Chapter 12 of the NeWS manual, has been extended to handle digitized still frames of video. If *string* is (*VideoFrame*), the resulting canvas will be a full NTSC video frame, 640x482x8 in YUV format. If *string* is (*VideoField*), the resulting canvas will be an NTSC video field, 640x241x8 in YUV format. If *string* is (*VideoGreyFrame*), the resulting canvas will be a 640x482x5 greyscale canvas in graphics format.

channel **vsource** —

> sets the channel for the NTSC input to the board, which is then saved in the current graphics context. With a two input board, the values 0 and 1 are valid.

9.2.3 NeWS Programming Examples

This section gives some examples of how to use these video capabilities. First, a video window must be created. This is accomplished by calling the /**new** method of the *VideoWindow* class:

```
framebuffer /new VideoWindow send
```

This code fragment creates an instance of the *VideoWindow* class and leaves it on the stack. The parent window is the display. The following fragment will perform the same operation, but will associate the instance with a name by which it can be referred:

```
/win framebuffer /new VideoWindow send def
```

The video window can now be referenced by the name *win*. Next, let the user pick size and placement of the window so that it can be displayed:

```
/reshapefromuser win send
```

The **reshapefromuser** operation is normally performed for any window class (see other examples in Chapter 6). Once it has been executed, a window of type **Video** is displayed on the screen. In order to display live video in this window, it must have a NeWS *PaintClient* procedure. This procedure will be executed any time the window is damaged. (It should be noted that mapping a window causes it to be damaged, so the last step performed above left the window in a damaged state.) The following is an example *PaintClient* procedure that displays live video:

```
/PaintClient {
    gsave       Save graphics state.
    newpath clipcanvas
                Reset the canvas clip.
    initclip clippath
                Set current path to the inside of the window.
    vstop       Stop previous live video.
    2 0 0 vstart
                Start video.
    grestore
                Restore graphics state.
} def
```

In order to make this example run, the *PaintClient* procedure must be passed to the window before it is mapped. The calls were presented in a different sequence in order to make the process less confusing. Here is the complete sequence of steps necessary to display a live video window:

```
/win framebuffer /new VideoWindow send def
{
    /PaintClient {
        gsave
        newpath clipcanvas
        initclip clippath
        vstop
        2 0 0 vstart
        grestore
    } def
} win send
/reshapefromuser win send
/map win send
```

Now that the basic sequence of steps has been covered, the following examples will present the *PaintClient* procedure itself. Here we fill a window with a frame of still video:

```
/PaintClient{
    gsave       Save graphics state.
    newpath clipcanvas
                Reset the canvas clip.
    640 480 scale
                Original size of frame.
    (VideoFrame) readcanvas
    imagecanvas
    grestore Restore graphics state.
} def
```

Note that the canvas clip is always reset, so that the entire canvas will be redrawn regardless of the damage that occurs to the window. The reason for this is that if the current source of video is constantly changing, care must be taken to ensure that information from a single frame is always displayed. Otherwise, if part of a window is covered and then uncovered, the uncovered part would be drawn with information from a different frame.

In order to fill a window with a video frame, regardless of the window size, the video information must be scaled proportionally to the window size. The scaling is implemented by the following code:

```
/PaintClient{
    gsave       Save graphics state.
    newpath clipcanvas
                Reset the canvas clip.
    intitclip clippath
                Set the current path to the inside of the window.
      pathbbox scale
                Scale to fit the window.
    pop pop
                Pathbbox gave us two extra numbers - get rid of them.
    (VideoFrame) readcanvas imagecanvas
    grestore Restore graphics state.
} def
```

Because NeWS treats video canvases in much the same way as normal graphics canvases, creating graphics overlays is straightforward:

```
/PaintClient{
    gsave       Save graphics state.
    newpath clipcanvas
                Reset the canvas clip.
    intitclip clippath
                Set the current path to the inside of the window.
    pathbbox scale
                Scale to fit the window.
    pop pop    Pathbbox gave us two extra numbers - get rid of them.
    (VideoFrame) readcanvas imagecanvas
                Fill window with video.
```

```
(Times-Bold) findfont 36 scalefont setfont
```
       Pick our font.
```
initmatrix 10 70 moveto

(Text is easy over video) show

grestore
```
Restore graphics state.
```
} def
```

Creating overlays on live video would be just as simple.

9.2.4 The VideoDisk Browser

To show the power of this addition to the NeWS server, this section includes some example code segments cut out of a real application, the "Video Disk Map Browser". In this, a videodisk storing up to 54000 video frames each the equivalent of a 300Kb data file is attached to the workstation (its video output goes to the graphics board and its RS-232 control line goes to a serial port). The disk contains various maps of a specific area of the world at different scales. The maps are stored as a series of single frames on the video disk arranged as groups; one group for each map scale.

The object of the application is to allow a user to scan the mapping disk in a North/South/East/West direction as well as Zoom In/Out to control the scale of the map.

The user interface is designed to show all the information in one area of the screen, in contrast to the same application running on a computer terminal with a TV monitor next to it. By using the NeWS server, the application can be combined with other applications doing graphics on the same screen.

The Browser first opens a window and sets it to be a *VideoWindow*. The *Canvas* (and hence window) is then filled with a video frame. The Browser presents a set of labelled buttons (implemented with the *LiteItem* button package) to give the user control of the map. The user can move the map in the NORTH, SOUTH, EAST, WEST directions and ZOOM the map in and out by pressing the mouse button on the desired button.

The Browser contains both C and NeWS code. The C portion of the program deals with the disk database and also controls of the videodisk player via the RS-232 port. The NeWS code handles the display of video frames and also the mouse input. It also processes windowing events such as *redisplay* and *resize* without executing C code.

As with most NeWS applications, the Browser begins by creating a simple *PaintClient* procedure. This procedure redisplays both the current video frame and the buttons. A crosshair cursor is placed at the center of the screen with the coordinates shown as text.

```
/current-video { % => canvas
    (VideoFrame) readcanvas
} def
/repaint-video {
    gsave
    initgraphics
    clippath pathbbox clipcanvas
    clippath pathbbox scale pop pop
    current-video imagecanvas
    grestore
} def

/PaintClient {
    repaint-video
    repaint-buttons
    repaint-coordinate
} def
```

The *repaint-video* routine takes the present video input and fills the whole window with it. The video input scales to fit. The C code that interacts with this NeWS fragment is:

```
main()
{
    char which[132];

    ps_open_PostScript();
    ps_initialize();

    getframe(0, 0);
    while (1) {
        ps_button(which)
        switch(which[0]) {
        case 'N':
            getframe(0, 1);
            break;
        case 'E':
            ....

getframe(deltax, deltay)
    ...
    ps_newframe(x, y);
```

The C routine *getframe()* takes care of all database interaction, and will call the NeWS routine *ps_newframe* when a new video input is available.

The *ps_newframe* is defined in the *cps* file so that it can be called directly from the C code. This procedure sends a redisplay event to the window when a new video input is available:

```
cdef ps_newframe(x, y)
    /current-x x store
    /current-y y store
    /paintclient win send
```

A listing of the final NeWS Browser Code can be obtained through the *news-archive@sun* network archive server. See Section 8.12 for more information on how to use news-archive@sun.

The complete application contains additional NeWS programs that allow video frames to be stored offscreen and used as a video disk cache. The caching facility enables a user to look at a previously-viewed frame (a common operation) without re-accessing the disk, allowing a substantial improvement in interactive performance.

9.2.5 Conclusion

The use of standard video in a windowing environment greatly expands the scope and quality of window-based applications by removing many of the restrictions in the way visual information is acquired, processed, and presented. NeWS provides a flexible software platform upon which sophisticated multi-media applications can be built on powerful computer workstations. Integrating video display with NeWS allows the combination of their full graphics, windowing, processing, and networking power with one of the most widely used and effective communication technologies.

9.3   Porting NeWS to the SGI IRIS

Silicon Graphics Computer Systems, Inc. manufactures the IRIS family of high-performance, high-resolution, color workstations for 2- and 3-dimensional graphics. The heart of the IRIS is a custom VLSI chip called the *Geometry Engine*. A pipeline of several Geometry Engines accepts points, vectors, polygons, and curves in user-defined coordinate systems, and transforms them to screen coordinates with the use of rotation, scaling and clipping.

Conceptually the graphics hardware of the IRIS is divided into three pipelined components: the applications processor, the geometry pipeline, and the raster subsystem.

The applications processor runs the applications program and controls the geometry pipeline and raster subsystem. Graphics routines are expressed in either 2-D or 3-D user coordinates. These coordinates pass through the geometry pipeline which transforms and clips them to normalized coordinates then scales the normalized coordinates to screen or window coordinates with a lower-left origin.

The pipeline output passes to the raster subsystem, which fills in the pixels between the endpoints of the lines and interiors of the polygons, and performs shading, depth-cueing, and hidden surface removal. A color value for each pixel is stored in the bit planes. An additional set of *overlay* bit planes is provided for transient displays such as pop-up menus. The overlay bit planes are displayed over the image in the main bit planes.

For several years the IRIS family has used a proprietary window system called *mex*. *mex* is typical of many early window systems in that the window manager (the policy) is inextricably linked with the window system (the mechanism). *mex*'s policy is all but impossible to change. *mex* is also very simple. It cannot, for example, close a window into an icon.

SGI wants to provide an environment on the IRIS that is not only more productive for the developer, but also encourages the developer to write applications that operate inside that environment. This focus benefits the end-user who can then mix and match applications to fill his needs. Currently many developers ignore *mex*, resulting in unsociable applications that take over the whole machine.

SGI would have to undertake a major rewrite of *mex* to provide the facilities commonly expected of window systems today. The benefits of such a major investment in reinventing the wheel were questionable. SGI customers would benefit most from an open, network-based window system. Such a system makes a wider range of applications and productivity tools available to them, as well as bringing the benefits of network transparency to (at least 2-D) applications.

After examining the alternatives, SGI selected NeWS primarily because of the PostScript language imaging model. NeWS clients use of their own coordinate space, the built in transformations, the consequent lack of intimacy with pixels and the default lower-left origin closely mirror the IRIS hardware model. SGI was also attracted by the potential for avoiding exclusive-OR operations provided by the overlay canvas paradigm. Exclusive-OR is not an efficient operation on certain IRIS models.

The boundless flexibility offered by the programmable server and lightweight processes added to its appeal. NeWS' ability to provide a global user-interface style that can be modified, even while NeWS is running and without any changes to the applications, is an attractive feature. Clients, too, can change their interfaces while remaining within the window system framework.

This flexibility is beneficial to both end-users and software developers. End-users benefit because they can change anything from presentation details to the complete window manager. Software developers benefit because they can change the user-interface details to suit the needs of their applications, yet those applications can still be sociable. On the other hand, they need to exercise self-restraint or the result will be chaos.

9.3.1 The Port(s)

SGI first ported NeWS to an IRIS 3030. The 3030 comes with 8 or 24 bit planes, and uses a 68020 as its applications processor. It operates in one graphics mode at a time: color-index mode (*cmode*) or RGB mode. The window system runs in cmode as most applications are written in that mode. The 3030 uses UNIX System V Release 0.

Our first copy of NeWS, an early pre-release version, came directly from the developer's source hierarchy and lacked documentation. NeWS was designed to be portable, but browsing the Sun development source reinforced the lesson that isolating system-specific dependencies is difficult. We discovered non-portable aspects including: long file names, dependencies on a 4.2BSD UNIX *stdio* (standard input and output) package, 4.2BSD *signals*, and the use of some non-standard C language extensions such as left-hand casts. Fortunately, interprocess communication, the hardest potential problem, was already solved. The IRIS uses the 4.3BSD networking code so the reliance of the Sun-specific NeWS code on sockets was not an issue. We were assured that the next release, the first real beta release, would be portable. The current version of NeWS is indeed very portable.

SGI split into two groups to focus our efforts: one to deal with compilation issues, the other to study the graphics. We planned to modify the graphics code to call Silicon Graphics Remote Graphics Library, *RGL*. The RGL calls would be sent to an IRIS for remote imaging. Ultimately these calls would be converted to calls to the standard Silicon Graphics' Graphics Library (*GL*).

In view of the promised portable source, we left the long file names alone and compiled, via the Network File System (NFS), from the source on our Sun. The left-hand casts were among the most difficult problems to fix and some of the NeWS expressions were too complex for our compiler.

The RGL work had succeeded in rendering window outlines by the time we first compiled NeWS on an IRIS. Initial examination of the standard imaging layer (an extended version of Sun's *pixrect* library) revealed that in order to take full advantage of our transformation hardware, we would, as Sun had warned, have to rewrite the entire imaging layer from the *cscript*[1] layer down to our hardware. All incoming coordinates pass through software transformations as soon as they arrive in the server. Only transformed coordinates are sent to the *pixrect*[2] layer, and these are in a screen space with an upper-left origin. Since we didn't have time to rewrite the imaging layer, we do not use the geometry pipeline for the PostScript language transformations. We do use it for the final inversion to IRIS screen space.

---

1. cscript is the interface between the PostScript interpreter and the imaging layer of the server.
2. pixrects are the bottom layer of the imaging section of the version 1.1 server.

Our first graphics implementation used a version of a memory pixrect that wrote to the screen any pixel that was modified by a RasterOp. This took about a week to get running. We implemented both color and monochrome versions. Of course it was fairly slow and used lots of memory, but it worked. We then turned our attention to input.

Input presented special issues. On the IRIS, keyboard and mouse events are delivered via a shared memory *gl queue*. It was impossible to *select* on this queue. Furthermore, the events did not contain timestamps. To solve this problem, we added an extra keyboard and mouse to our development systems, plugged into *tty* ports. We then wrote a version of the operating system interface that read the serial ports and created the NeWS events. This arrangement gave us enough input for selection and typing a few characters to *psterm*.

Our ultimate twofold solution to the input problem necessitated kernel changes. We created a pseudo-device */dev/queue* that *selects* when an event is in the process's *gl* queue. This pseudo-device will be useful to many IRIS applications. We also created a new shared memory queue that accommodates timestamps. This queue is for keyboard and mouse events only and a process must be registered as the window manager to use it. When enabled, the shared-memory queue becomes the target of selects on /dev/queue.

With input problems behind us, our attention returned to imaging. We reworked the pixrect implementation case-by-case to use the GL and take every advantage of the hardware. The first change was the re-implementation of *fill* in the RasterOp routine. The re-implementation had a dramatic positive effect on performance. A great deal of the PostScript language imaging is accomplished at the lowest level with fills. Once all pixrect cases had been tackled, we removed the shadow memory needed for the memory pixrect implementation.

To take further advantage of our hardware we wanted to use the hardware cursor and to change the overlay canvas implementation to use the overlay planes rather than exclusive-OR. We also wanted to put the menus in the overlay planes to avoid having to read back the pixels under them, a relatively slow operation on certain IRIS models.

Making NeWS use the hardware cursor was straightforward. We simply changed the macros *cv_cursor_up* and *cv_cursor_down* to be no-ops and wrote a function that loads a cursor glyph into the hardware whenever the function *cs_newcursor* is called. We also modified the graphics microcode to support a two-color cursor.

The overlay canvas implementation required significant modification. The standard NeWS server implements overlay canvases by storing a display list, and traversing the display list, whenever the cursor is drawn, painting the primitives in XOR mode. Supporting menus requires at least two colors in the overlay canvas rather than the single "invert" color. As the overlay canvas no longer needed to be drawn and erased when the cursor moved, we changed the imaging routines to draw as soon as a request came in, as well as inserting it into the display list, and modified *cv_unmap* to actually unmap an overlay canvas. We retained the display list because it is much faster to erase lines than fill the planes with transparent color.

We also enhanced the menu package by creating a transparent canvas to give us the hit detection, and then imaging the menu in an overlay canvas on top of that. No damage would then be caused to the underlying canvas.

By now we were comfortable with NeWS. We had a solid, well running implementation. With a stable NeWS server in hand it was time to port NeWS to two more members of the IRIS family: the IRIS 4D/70G and the IRIS 4D/70GT. The 4D/70G's applications processor is a MIPS R2000 RISC processor. It has an enhanced version of the pipeline architecture that is faster and allows multiple simultaneous graphics modes. The IRIS 4D/70GT couples the same R2000 processor with a brand new very high-performance pipeline architecture that is an order of magnitude faster than the earlier design[AKEL88]. It is capable of rendering up to 100,000 quadrilaterals per second. Both machines run UNIX System V Release 3.

The 4D/70G port was the first that we tackled.

The MIPS architecture proved a bigger hurdle than the new graphics. It requires that data fetches be aligned on their natural boundaries. For example, an *int* must be fetched from an address that is modulo 4. Because of this, we had to rewrite large portions of the pixrect code that assumed fetching an int from any even address would work. We faced a major problem with the way NeWS implements the pointers to a PostScript object's body. Every PostScript object is represented by a C data structure, *struct object*. Large objects (e.g. dicts) with bodies have a field in their *struct object* that points to a C data structure representing the body. There are many objects, and it is important to keep the *struct object* small. To this end, NeWS allocates only 26 bits to the pointer, masking off the other bits in the word before using the pointer. The MIPS CPU needs 29 bits for this pointer; we tried both adding the extra (constant) bits before using the pointer, and making *struct object* larger to accommodate the extra bits before settling on the former.

Since the 4D/70G supports multiple simultaneous graphics modes and is typically configured with 24 bitplanes, we modified the NeWS server to do full 24-bit RGB imaging. The major work here was implementing the functions supporting *readcanvas* and *imagecanvas*. There is no noticeable difference in performance between the 8- and 24-bit models.

We tired of the simplicity of *LiteWindow*, so we created a new *SGIWindow* subclass with a different appearance and feel. This took only about eight hours, giving us a clear demonstration of the power of NeWS extensibility and the efficacy of NeWS programming classes.

9.3.2   Integration

We were now ready to integrate NeWS into our system. Integration work began while the MIPS port was being finished.

Graphics applications on the IRIS (called GL clients) draw by calling Graphics Library routines that make direct drawing requests to the hardware. When they operate in a windowed environment an outside agent sets up clipping hardware to ensure the GL client is confined to its windows. For NeWS to become the controlling window system for the IRIS it had to take over the job of setting up the hardware clipping from *mex* and also the job of initializing the hardware. A major goal was that an application would only need re-linking to work under NeWS therefore we needed to mimic the old *mex* programming interface.

We wrote a subclass of SGIWindow called *MEXWindow* with all the behavior of the old *mex* windows. We then created an identical function call interface which was added to the GL. An important part of MEXWindow is a lightweight process that handles input events for the GL client. It expresses interest in NeWS events in response to *qdevice* calls from the GL. Matched events are translated to the GL format and placed in the client's *gl* queue.

To manage the hardware clipping we created the *GL canvas*. A GL canvas behaves for the most part just like a normal NeWS canvas, except that it cannot be drawn on with PostScript programs. The GL canvas reserves space on the screen for the GL client and provides a convenient place to store information needed to manage clipping and to communicate with the client.

The 4D/70G clips to a rectangle list that is equivalent to the visible region of the GL canvas. Whenever that region changes we must reload the *piecelist* as it is known. There are two cases to handle here: uncovering and covering a canvas. When a canvas is uncovered damage is caused as with NeWS canvases. MEXwindow responds to the /**Damaged** event by requesting the damagepath before sending a REDRAW event to the GL client. The piecelist is updated at this point.

Because the GL client is drawing asynchronously to the server, we must reset the piecelist as soon as a GL canvas is about to be covered. Normally at this point NeWS merely invalidates the canvas's clipping. It is validated again when the client makes its next drawing request. Resetting the piecelist whenever we invalidate the clip requires validating it again immediately, which is a time-consuming operation. Typically NeWS iterates through the about-to-be-covered fragments of a canvas, calling **cv_invalidateclip** for each fragment. Setting the piecelist each time would therefore be very inefficient. Instead we added a *reclip* list which is very similar to the damage queue. The reclip list is checked after NeWS has iterated through a list of about-to-be-covered fragments and the piecelist for any canvas in the reclip list is reset.

On the 4D/70GT clipping is done against a mask painted into special *window ID* planes. Clipping to arbitrary shapes is done with no performance degradation. The window ID planes are much easier to manage than piecelists. Uncovering of canvases is handled using the damage queue exactly like piecelists. When a canvas is to be covered the window ID planes at that location are painted to establish clipping for the canvas that is to appear. This automatically clips the canvas being covered.

One of the last areas we dealt with was the colormap. Some of our systems have only 8 bit planes, so we needed the NeWS colormap. For compatibility we had to set the bottom 8 colors to the standard SGI colors and wanted the greyramp next. To accommodate the eight colors we shrank the greyramp and placed it after the standard colors. Color 0 is black which caused a problem in retained canvases when *mem_rop* expands a source pixrect from *1*-bits to *n*-bits.

9.3.3   Conclusion

Building on top of the GL canvases and the GL client interface, we have added an X11 server that runs alongside NeWS and sociably shares the screen with the NeWS window manager in control. The color plate[1] shows the complete IRIS Window System, known as *4sight*.

We are looking forward to the X11/NeWS merge and to improving the imaging layer implementation to fully reflect the match between the PostScript language imaging model and our pipeline hardware. We naturally want to explore 3-D extensions to the PostScript language and merging our Distributed Graphics Library with the *4sight* window server.

9.4   Architech Corporation: NeWS/2

Architech's NeWS/2 is a port of Sun's NeWS to Microsoft's OS/2 environment for the IBM-PC and PC-compatible microcomputers.

This initial release of NeWS/2 is a monochrome implementation that communicates with client applications using the OS/2 LAN Manager's named pipes. It includes all of the development tools and demonstration programs distributed with Sun's NeWS product.

NeWS/2 also provides VIO-Term, a facility in which unmodified OS/2 character-based applications can execute in a NeWS window.

9.4.1   Background

Creating a NeWS port for the OS/2 environment was an appealing challenge for several reasons. First, from Architech's perspective, OS/2 is the first "true" operating system to become available for personal computers.

1. The color plates appear immediately after p. 222—see Appendix I, Description of the Plates.

Unlike DOS or the Macintosh Finder, OS/2 provides features such as multi-tasking and virtual memory. Surprisingly coherent and well thought-out, it incorporates such NeWS-compatible philosophies as lightweight processes (threads) and shared packages (e.g., DynaLink Libraries.)

Second, the official user interface for OS/2 — Presentation Manager (PM) — does not reflect new user interface technology, but is very dependent on the previous MSWindows user interface and window system, which had some integral limitations. In addition, the Presentation Manager is complex to program, and offers little new in terms of window technology. NeWS, on the other hand, offers a radically new, "second-generation" approach to user interface development.

A third factor was the importance of timing. Offering an alternative to the Presentation Manager was timely, since OS/2 developers have not yet invested significant resources in Presentation Manager development. Developers are not yet dependent upon these interfaces, and there are times when standards exist for the benefit of exceptions. And finally, it makes business sense for Architech to bring technology like NeWS to a large market; the OS/2 market forecasts sales of 4 million units per year by 1991. The availability of NeWS on both UNIX and OS/2 is of great interest to developers trying to maximize their potential markets.

9.4.2 Technical Aspects

Architech found that the technical problems usually accompanying a port were significantly reduced by the excellent job done by Sun's portable NeWS group. Prior to releasing NeWS source to licensees, virtually all of the OS and byte ordering dependencies had already been clearly delineated or moved to separate files. Yet despite the best efforts of everyone involved, a few troublesome items remained. One notable item was the existence of file names that were slightly too long for the OS/2 environment. This problem, a nuisance in the best of circumstances, became especially burdensome when the slightly-too-long file name was the name of a header file that could be found virtually everywhere within the code. Other technical problems we encountered included unportable C pre-processor tricks, 32-bit integers, and extra-large C files (truly, extra-large C files: 82K bytes, for example).

Architech decided early on that there were two possible strategies for dealing with these problems: either the entire source could be cross-compiled from the SUN to 80286 code and then linked on the PC, or a set of custom tools to do the job directly under OS/2 could be developed. They opted for the tools; developing a C pre-processor and a cross-referencer.

The C pre-processor automatically converted invalid file names, did the "expected" thing with unportable macro constructs, and was able to handle an arbitrary amount of pre-processor statements.

The cross-referencer kept track of the large number of macros used in the NeWS source, and alerted the programmer when a statement in the source code was a macro rather than simply a function call.

Some of the major sources of new code in the NeWS/2 port were the Sun *pixrect* library, which had to be written for EGA/VGA hardware; the implementation in OS/2 of some unavailable UNIX functionality; and a new memory management algorithm designed to be efficient within a segment swapping architecture.

The *pixrect* library implementation was quite straightforward, and did not require any special OS/2 features. The UNIX compatibility functions, on the other hand, required some unexpected work. For example, two UNIX system calls central to the NeWS architecture are *select()* and *fcntl()*. The plain-vanilla *open()*, *read()*, *write()*, and *close()* functions of most OS/2 C libraries are inadequate for this sort of use, and had to be re-implemented using lower level OS/2 functions. Similarly, the UNIX socket model had to be partially simulated with OS/2 named pipes. Specifically, the security features present in the original BSD sockets were not completely reimplemented in the OS/2 port, since real sockets will be made available in the near future.

The memory management algorithm is discussed in the section on big segment swapping, below.

9.4.3 NeWS/2 Limitations

NeWS/2 is a fully functional port of NeWS to the OS/2 environment. However, the fact that OS/2 is designed to work on a 80286 16-bit CPU (even, alas, when NeWS/2 is running on an 80386 chip machine) introduces two specific hardware limitations. These limitations are discussed below.

9.4.3.1 Puny Segments vs. Enormous Arrays

The segmented architecture of the 80286 imposes a 64-Kilobyte (K) limit on the size of any contiguous memory area. This restriction hinders NeWS/2 functionality in only one case: very large arrays. The NeWS limit is 32,000 objects per array; the NeWS/2 limit, on the other hand, is only some 5000 objects per array. Such large arrays are rather rare, but they do occur. One such occurrence, for example, is in the very complex pictures which can be generated by some drawing applications (e.g., large Adobe Illustrator files), which are represented as gigantic executable arrays.

To work properly in the NeWS/2 port, the files generated by such programs have to be cut by hand in smaller chunks. The vast executable array that was originally generated is thus replaced by smaller arrays, which can then be executed in the body of the original.

To further minimize this problem, a future release of NeWS/2 will have the ability to automatically "chop up" such large executable arrays. When an OS/2 for the 80386 chip arrives, of course, the problem will go away entirely.

9.4.3.2   Big Segment Swapping

Virtual memory management on the 80286 (and, again, on the 80386 under the present version of OS/2) uses segment swapping. While these segments can vary in size from 1 byte to 64K bytes, they are always swapped to disk in one chunk. Regular heap memory management algorithms make the segment swapping virtually useless; such algorithms tend to allocate memory into 64K segments, which are then divided into smaller chunks as requested by *malloc()* or *calloc()*. Later, when a *free()* call returns such a chunk to the heap, the chunk is added to some free memory chunk list.

The result is twofold: (1) most segments are 64K in size, and (2) the free list(s) criss-cross these large segments. When memory becomes over-committed and some segments have to be moved to disk, entire 64K segments are swapped out (rather than a 2 or 4K page as in a Virtual Paging system). Worse, when *malloc()* is called (a frequent occurrence) and some free list is traversed, several 64K segments have to be swapped in and out several times.

The result — the disk drive access light flickers on and off as it would in a system crash — is unacceptable.

To deal effectively with this problem, it was necessary to rewrite the memory-management routines to use 4K segments, with one free list per segment, and a single list of segments. If an extra-large chunk of memory needs to be allocated, a specially fitted segment is created by the memory-management routine. The resulting change has been phenomenal: now, even when the system swap file becomes larger than the core memory space, there is almost no degradation of performance.

9.4.4   Using NeWS in OS/2

Although OS/2 and UNIX are similar in many ways, OS/2 features (and therefore OS/2 applications) are not always UNIX-like. For example, UNIX applications most often communicate through their standard I/O file descriptors: even when the applications are full-screen, they use ANSI-like serial protocols to manage their output. Under OS/2, however, and as a legacy from the unruly reign of DOS, character-based applications can use either standard I/O (as in UNIX), or an OS/2 character-based user interface library called VIO, which allows fast full-screen control through the use of function calls.

Since the VIO library, however, expects direct access to the entire screen as well as control of the keyboard, it would obviously have to be replaced in a windowed environment such as NeWS. To deal with this problem, NeWS/2 provides an application called VIO-Term, which "registers" (that is, selectively replaces) the VIO library. Since VIO is a DynaLink library, it is not attached to applications at link time but rather at load time, and thus can be replaced without having to relink the applications that use it. The VIO-Term opens a NeWS window, and the original VIO calls are translated into equivalent PostScript language code.

This resulting VIO Window is interesting for at least three reasons. First, because VIO-Term is a DynaLink Library that attaches itself to client applications, no modifications to the NeWS server nor its initialization files are required. Second, character-based OS/2 applications, without the need for any modification, now become networkable a là NeWS.

Finally, not only the VIO subsystem, but the entire Presentation Manager, can be replaced. Hence, any Presentation Manager application could run unmodified in the NeWS environment. These PM applications could even have their output sent over a network to a Sun screen.

Another OS/2 feature which becomes especially intriguing to the developer of NeWS-based applications is preemptive light-weight processes, or "threads", on the client side.

The concept of having one thread reading and dispatching input from the NeWS server while another thread is collecting and sending output to the same server was so attractive that we adapted the *cps* library to this preemptive environment. The adaptation involved a small semaphore-like operation in the PSIO code of the *cps* library, which was necessary to avoid untimely flushes of the output stream by the input thread. The result is totally transparent.

Still, *cps* lacks features which would allow a multithreaded application to communicate freely with lightweight NeWS mechanisms. For example, a multithreaded environment *cps* would allow PostScript pipes to be multiplexed, or, at the very least, would allow one client to have several connections to the NeWS server simultaneously. As multithreading becomes widely used (under UNIX as well as OS/2), it will make sense for *cps* to grow in that direction.

OS/2 also provides "sessions," a mechanism by which several applications can take full control of the screen. Each application has total control during the period of time it resides in the foreground of the screen. When the application is switched to the background (usually by a user command from the keyboard), OS/2 takes care of preserving both the screen hardware state and its contents. The application is only responsible for stopping output while it resides in the background, or for holding that output in a separate "virtual screen," later restoring this virtual screen to the real screen when the user brings the application to the foreground again. The session mechanism allows different user interface technologies such as NeWS and Presentation Manager to coexist on the same machine, without having to be aware of each other and without limiting each other. This versatility is a far cry from the days of DOS.

9.4.5 Future Enhancements and Conclusion

Architech intend to keep NeWS/2 as closely compatible as possible with Sun's future releases, and will offer the X11/NeWS server, described in the next chapter, as soon as feasible.

Furthermore, although they hope that future Sun NeWS releases will include some preemptive process switching, they plan to incorporate the necessary code on their own if Sun chooses not to.

Architech's approach will involve semi-preemptive process switching via a simulated "pause" statement generated whenever some user-defined timer goes off. This will allow the user to set the context switching granularity, or even to remove it altogether. Also, such time-consuming operations as dithering, scaling, and the rotation of large pixrects will be done by background threads, while other NeWS processes keep running.

Finally, Architech also intends to provide OPEN LOOK and the OPEN LOOK NeWS Development Environment (NDE) as soon as Sun and AT&T make them available. They see a NeWS-based OPEN LOOK user interface as an attractive choice for OS/2 users and developers.

10
X11/NeWS Design Overview

"No group's talent
Could be the equivalent
Of mine and his combined;
Total harmony between the cuts and the rhyme."
LL Cool J, *Dangerous*

10.1 Introduction

The X window system development at MIT defined an important standard protocol for window system development: the Version 11 protocol. (The evolution and structure of the X window system are described in Chapter 3.) The industry interest in X11, the PostScript language, and NeWS resulted in the definition of a combined window server architecture: the X11/NeWS merge. Combining the X11 fixed protocol with an enhanced PostScript language, together with the dynamic development environment of NeWS, gives the applications developer a synthesis of standards, functionality, and flexibility[ROBE88].

10.2 Goals

The goal of the merge of X11 and NeWS is to produce a single server process that supports the entire semantics of both the X11 and NeWS protocols, allows a single window manager to control all windows, and supports portable X11 extensions. This server should be portable to a wide variety of hardware.

If the X11/NeWS server is to support both NeWS and X11 clients, it must correctly implement the semantics of both protocols. Some of the design challenges are discussed below.

Applications built to both window protocols must run side-by-side on the screen and present an integrated interface to the user. Thus, a single window manager must manage all windows regardless of the protocol used to create them. A window manager that uses the NeWS protocol can manage windows that were created by either X11 or NeWS clients. Window managers written to use the X11 protocol can manage windows created by X11 clients, but can only manage windows created by NeWS clients that follow the rules of the X11 protocol.

The X11 protocol specification[SCHE87] defines a means of extending the X11 protocol. The existing MIT sample server implementation provides a mechanism for implementing extensions, documented in the *X11 Server Extensions Engineering Specification*[FISH87]. While the latter mechanism is still under development, the intention is that extension implementations that use it will be portable across X11 server implementations. X11/NeWS supports portable X11 extensions in the following sense. The extension specification requires that a small set of include files and the source to one procedure be provided with the server. Without any other source, an extension supplier should be able to recompile a portable extension with the X11/NeWS *include* files, link it with X11/NeWS object libraries, and have the extension work.

10.3   Architecture

A server for either protocol must perform three major functions:

Scheduling interpretation of protocol requests.

Allocation of portions of the display.

Distribution of input.

Figure 10.1 shows the structure of the X11/NeWS server, an architecture that provides these functions for both X11 and NeWS. If the X11 client and interpreter were omitted, this figure would illustrate the structure of the existing NeWS server. If the NeWS client and interpreter were omitted, it would illustrate the structure of the X11 sample server from MIT.

In Figure 10.1, the boxes labelled **X** represent interpretation or generation of X11 protocol, and the boxes labelled **N** represent interpretation or generation of NeWS protocol. The boxes in the area labelled **window forest** represent *windows* (called *canvases* in NeWS), which are portions of the screen on which clients can draw. The unlabelled windows in the diagram could have been created by either protocol; the protocol used to create them does not affect the structure of the window forest or the structure of the windows themselves. The boxes in the area labelled **event queue** represent events, and are likewise unlabelled because the protocol used by the recipient of the events is irrelevant to event queuing and distribution.

10.3.1 The Scheduler

Given multiple clients of a window server, a way must be provided to fairly and predictably schedule execution of requests from each. Allocation of time between multiple clients is required of all X11 servers, and all NeWS servers; therefore it is also required of the X11/NeWS server.

NeWS schedules between lightweight processes. As described in Chapter 5, a process is a thread of control; a lightweight process is a process which shares its address space with other lightweight processes. In NeWS, a context switch may occur when a lightweight process blocks or explicitly gives up control. In contrast, X11 schedules between clients. In X11, a context switch may occur between any two requests, unless a client has grabbed the server.

An X11 client is a source of a sequence of X11 requests. A sequence of X11 requests is a linear thread of control. Since a linear thread of control is a subset of the possibilities offered by a process, the X11/NeWS server represents X11 clients as lightweight processes.

Context switching and scheduling are entirely internal to the X11/NeWS server and are not dependent on the operating system. An X11/NeWS lightweight process is represented as a context structure, whose contents include the protocol interpreter associated with that lightweight process, and the source of protocol to be interpreted. The source of protocol may be a client connection or downloaded code.

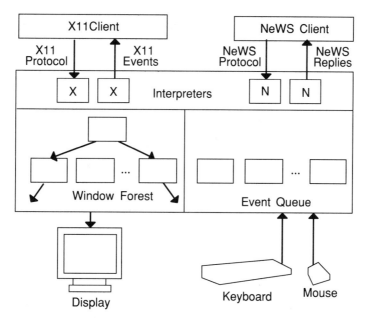

Figure: 10.1.   X11/NeWS server architecture.

Running a lightweight process means calling the associated interpreter procedure and passing in the context structure for the lightweight process. The interpreter checks a single state field in the context structure to resume where it left off when it last gave up control. As it executes, the interpreter maintains state in the context structure. To give up control, the lightweight process saves a value in the state field that it checked earlier when it resumed execution, and returns to the scheduler.

The scheduler makes no distinction with regard to the protocol interpreter associated with a lightweight process. A lightweight process runs until it gives up control, and is run again when it is ready.

10.4   Windows and Graphics in X11 and NeWS

10.4.1 Sharing a Screen

NeWS and X11 are very similar in the way that they treat the screen. Both allocate portions of the screen on which a client can draw, called *canvases* in NeWS, and *windows* in X11. (From here on, these terms will be used interchangeably. Detailed discussion of canvases and their relationship to windows is discussed in Chapters 5 and 6.) Both X11 and NeWS permit unlimited nesting and overlapping of windows. Both provide for expression of interest in events occurring on specific windows, including damage (exposure) and device input.

The X11/NeWS server has a tree of nested windows for each screen. The aggregate of these trees is called a *forest*. The server allows the cursor to roam across screens, in some device dependent geometry. An extension to the NeWS protocol for getting the list of screens is provided.

The structure underlying a node in the forest is called a *canvas* for historical reasons. The forest of canvases in the X11/NeWS server is homogeneous. The same canvas structure is used to represent both canvases created from NeWS protocol and windows created from X11 protocol. Since the forest is homogeneous, if a canvas is reconfigured to expose regions of underlying canvases, damage will be detected on all of them whether they were created using NeWS or X11 protocol.

NeWS canvases and X11 windows do have some differences. They provide different attributes, imaging models, color models, and font models. A more detailed description of how these differences are resolved in the X11/NeWS server is given below.

10.4.2 Properties

Each X11 window has a property list. NeWS canvases do not currently have property lists, but will benefit from such an addition. Canvases appear to NeWS programs as PostScript dictionaries; fields of a canvas appear as keys in the dictionary that represents it. NeWS programs can access the property list for a canvas through a new key in the canvas dictionary.

X11 Properties are quadruples - *name*, *type*, *format*, *data*:

name and *type*
> Both of these elements are X11 atoms, which map well onto the PostScript language **name** type.

format
> The format describes the unit size of *data*, which can be 8, 16, or 32 bits.

data
> This element consists of data that is handled but not interpreted by the server. It is represented by a NeWS string, which is essentially an array of 8-bit bytes. 16 and 32 bit format are implemented by having a string that is a multiple of 2 or 4 bytes long.

A property is constructed by combining the above elements into a four element array of in the order of name, type, format, and data.

A property list is an unordered set of properties. The most convenient data type in PostScript language for unordered sets is a dictionary, which is essentially a hash table. The property name serves as the key to a property.

10.4.3 Display Attributes

Although X11 and NeWS have many display attributes in common, there are a number of display attributes that are only accessible through one protocol or the other.

For example, X11 windows have borders, background, and gravity. These attributes allow an X11 server to immediately tidy the screen after a change to the window hierarchy without the overhead of a server-client round trip. In NeWS, downloaded PostScript code is used to perform display update functions that need instant response like these, and NeWS has no need of these attributes. In X11/NeWS, the window attributes are implemented by enhancing the canvas data structure and operations.

For another example, NeWS protocol provides access to a canvas' arbitrary shape, which is not necessarily rectangular. As X11 core protocol defines only rectangular windows, it only provides access to a canvas' bounding box. If an X11 client gets a handle on a non-rectangular canvas and inquires about the size and origin, it receives the bounding box of the canvas in the reply. If an X11 window is exposed by an operation on an occluding non-rectangular canvas, the exposed region is approximated (to the resolution of the display) by some number of rectangles.

10.4.4 Colormap Access

Although NeWS attempts to hide the details of the workstation's display hardware from clients, X11 tries to describe them. The X11 connection setup protocol specifies the pixel depth and colormap models available for each screen on the workstation in terms of *visual types*. One screen may have more than one visual type. For example, a framebuffer containing 8-bit deep color and an overlay plane offers a single screen with two visual types, one 8-bit PsuedoColor and one 1-bit StaticGray.

Each visual type supports the request **CreateColormap**. For static visual types (*StaticColor*, *StaticGray*, and *TrueColor*), **CreateColormap** returns the single static colormap provided by that visual type. For dynamic visual types (*PseudoColor*, *GrayScale*, and *DirectColor*), it returns a newly-created colormap. Each visual type has a default colormap, whose initial population of colors is not defined in the X11 protocol specification.

For devices that offer a hardware colormap, the X11/NeWS server populates part of the default colormap with read-only, sharable colors in the form of a colorcube whose axes are red, green, and blue. Doing so allows NeWS and X11 applications that do not require dynamic colormap access to share the colorcube. X11 applications needing dynamic colormap access either allocate colors from the rest of the default colormap, or allocate their own colormaps. An extension to NeWS provides dynamically modifiable colors in the rest of the colormap as well.

Each screen has some number of colormaps installed. When a colormap is installed, primitives drawn using pixels assigned from that map appear in their correct colors. When any application installs its own colormap, and the combined set of allocated colors overflows the hardware colormap, other applications (both NeWS and X11) appear wrong until their colormaps are reinstalled. The incorrect appearance is a problem in any implementation of X11 colormaps.

10.4.5 Imaging Model

NeWS is based upon the stencil-paint imaging model offered by the PostScript language. The stencil-paint imaging model reveals no notion of pixels, and allows a PostScript program to set up an arbitrary 2-D coordinate system (called world coordinates), whose units may be fractions of pixels. Even the default coordinate system need not be in units of screen pixels, as the PostScript language defines the default units to be 1/72 of an inch. Due to the arbitrary coordinate system, neither the stencil-paint imaging model nor the PostScript language make any guarantees about which pixels are touched when rendering the graphics primitives. (Sections 4.8 through 4.14 go into more detail about the way in which the PostScript language and NeWS implement the stencil-paint imaging model.)

Raising the level of abstraction from pixel coordinates to world coordinates has some advantages. If an image is described in world coordinates, switching from a low resolution to a high resolution device affects only image *quality*, not image *size*. This means that PostScript and NeWS programs transfer easily among radically different devices and the image quality merely increases as the devices increase in resolution or color capacity. Yet pixel, or actual device coordinates are still accessible by setting the transformation matrix to be the identity matrix, that is, by setting the world coordinate space to be the same as the device coordinate space. However, deferring the transformation of world coordinates into pixel coordinates to the server allows the server to utilize matrix multiplication hardware. Making no guarantees about which pixels to touch when rendering an image allows the server to utilize polygon, vector, and anti-aliasing hardware.

In contrast to NeWS, X11 specifies a pixel-based imaging model. Pixel coordinates are used throughout the X11 drawing operations. With the exception of *narrow* lines, (i.e., lines specified to have a width of zero), the X11 protocol specification describes rendering algorithms for all drawing primitives that guarantee pixel accuracy.

The X11 imaging model can be thought of as a precise specification of the pixels involved in drawing operations when the current transformation matrix is the identity matrix. If a graphics accelerator uses a different rendering algorithm from the algorithm specified by the X11 protocol, the X11 protocol specification requires the server to bypass the accelerator. If the server device drivers ignore the accelerator, both X11 and NeWS drawing operations can use the same rendering algorithms without loss of correctness or precision.

Operations defined in the X11 protocol, but not in NeWS, include *rasterops*, *tiling*, and *stencilling*. Similar operations are needed to implement the PostScript language imaging model on a bitmap display; they have been enhanced to support the X11 imaging model in the X11/NeWS server.

10.4.6 Fonts

Both NeWS and X11 currently support fonts described in Adobe Character Bitmap Distribution Format (*bdf*). These fonts are provided as ASCII files containing information about the family and face of the font followed by specific information and bitmaps for each of the characters in the font. NeWS and X11 each have a mechanism for converting these ASCII font files into a machine-dependent format suitable for efficient processing by the window system server. Figure 10.2 shows all the font files and utilities.

In the case of NeWS, ASCII font files are pre-processed by the dump-font utility to create binary font files consisting of a font structure followed by an array of structures, one for each character. For each font family, there also exists an ASCII font family description file, which is pre-processed by the *bldfamily* (build-family) utility to create a binary font family file. NeWS handles outline and stroked-font ASCII formats as well as bitmap fonts.

X11 uses a similar scheme to pre-process ASCII font files for subsequent loading in response to client requests, using the `fc` font compiler utility. These files consist of data structures containing font information, the glyphs themselves, and a number of font properties.

In X11/NeWS, both NeWS and X11 font requests are processed through an enhanced version of the existing NeWS font machinery. In the case of X11, font and glyph information, as derived from binary font files and maintained in NeWS data structures, are mapped to X11 data structures to be passed to the X11 interpreter as font requests are serviced. The X11/NeWS font file format and font compiler are upgraded to Version 2.1 of Adobe's Character Bitmap Distribution format. They are also enhanced to include X11 font information.

X11 assigns no format rules for font names, although it does follow certain naming conventions for groups of fonts. From the font name, the OS-dependent code generates the font file name for the file that contains the font. Any incompatibilities between NeWS-style and X11-style font names and font file names are resolved there.

But NeWS understands more than bitmap fonts. Fonts can be scan converted from intelligent spline outlines, or drawn by pieces of PostScript code. When an X11 application asks for a font, X11/NeWS parses the name by stripping off a trailing digit string, using it for a size, and interpreting the rest as a font name. So the X11 font "*Times-Roman12*" is interpreted as though it had been generated by the PostScript code fragment "/**Times-Roman findfont 12 scalefont**". This technique allows X11 applications to access a much wider selection of fonts under the merge.

10.5   Events

The primary difference between the X11 input model and the NeWS input model is that NeWS event distribution consists of message passing between lightweight processes within the server; whereas X11 event distribution consists of sending information to external clients. In the following discussion the term *client* is a lightweight process in NeWS and a client-side program in X11.

In spite of the major difference in input models, there are many points on which NeWS and X11 agree:

Events are collected from devices and timestamped as quickly as possible.

Events from all devices are serialized.

Events are normally delivered to clients in the order generated. Exceptions are X11 grabs and NeWS events whose timestamps are not the same as the time at which they were generated.

Clients indicate classes of events they wish to receive.

Events propagate up the window tree, but may be stopped explicitly by windows. Exceptions are X11 grabs and NeWS global interests.

Focus for keyboard events can be set explicitly.

Default mouse and keyboard input distribution follows the mouse.

Additionally, there are areas where X11 event distribution is a subset of NeWS event distribution:

NeWS events are perceived by PostScript programs as dictionaries; one event dictionary can carry all the information needed for X11 events.

NeWS interests are templates of the events or sets of events that match them. Such a template may be constructed for any set of events corresponding to any X11 interest mask bit.

10.5.1 Delivering Events to X11 Clients

In NeWS, PostScript programs form a bridge between the receipt of a NeWS event and the delivery of the information in that event to an external client. A PostScript program extracts relevant information from a NeWS event and writes it to the appropriate external connection.

In X11/NeWS, events are delivered to an X11 client by a lightweight process that waits for a NeWS event, then writes it in the form of an X11 event to its connection. As NeWS provides no mechanism for a lightweight process to block on two things at once, the lightweight process that blocks on a NeWS event is not the same one as the X11 interpreter lightweight process, which blocks on a connection read. The lightweight process that waits for events is called the *input agent*. The input agent is a NeWS program that runs in the server, but calls X11-specific primitives.

The conversion of NeWS events to X11 events has several advantages. First, an event may be put into the queue with no pre-established expectation of how it will ultimately be distributed. Second, both NeWS lightweight processes and X11 clients can receive the same events, improving the overall integration of the system.

Given that events are distributed to the input agent lightweight process, rather than the X11 interpreter lightweight process, interest in those events must be expressed by the input agent lightweight process. However, the X11 interpreter process receives the requests that set the client's interest. To reconcile this, the X11 interpreter process keeps a pointer to the input agent process, and adds appropriate interests to the input agent's interest list.

10.5.2 Event Distribution Within the Server

In NeWS, a lightweight process expresses interest in receiving particular events by creating a template event, known as an interest. Event distribution consists of searching the interests, using them as patterns to match the event against. For each interest matched by the event, a copy of the event is placed on the local queue of the lightweight process that expressed the matched interest. The NeWS **awaitevent** operator returns the top element, or the head, of the local queue.

An event may contain a canvas. In NeWS, when an event is expressed as an interest, if it contains a canvas, it is placed on that canvas' interest list, otherwise it is placed on a global interest list. The canvas hierarchy determines the order of the interest search during event distribution. When an event is distributed, if the event contains a canvas, only the interest list for that canvas is searched. Otherwise, the global interest list is searched, then the interest list of each canvas from the canvas under the mouse to the root is searched. The search is terminated:

If an exclusive interest is matched.

If an interest is matched on a canvas that consumes matched events.

If a canvas whose interest list was searched consumes all events.

The bottom-up distribution rule corresponds well to X11 device input distribution for most cases. The global-interest list serves active grabs well. However, the rules for X11 passive grabs (described later) correspond better to top-down distribution. Given the possibility of passive grabs, the event distribution rules have been generalized in X11/NeWS.

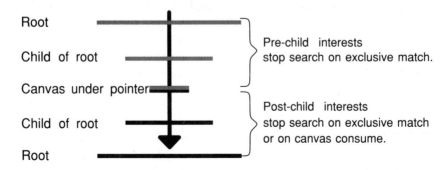

Figure: 10.2.   X11/NeWS event distribution process.

In X11/NeWS, each canvas has two interest lists, called *pre-child* and *post-child* interest lists. To distribute an event that specifies a canvas, the server searches the pre-child interest list of each canvas from the root to that canvas, then searches the post-child interest list of that canvas. To distribute an event that does not specify a canvas, the server searches the pre-child interest list of each canvas from the root to the canvas under the mouse, then searches the post-child interest list of each canvas from the canvas under the mouse to the root. Only a match of an exclusive interest can terminate the search on the way down. The old rules for terminating the search still apply on the way up. The global interest list is replaced by the pre-child interest list on the root canvas. Figure 10.2 illustrates the distribution process

The application of this general event distribution scheme to the various X11 input concepts is described below.

10.6   High Level X11 Concepts

The X11 protocol includes a number of concepts that are omitted from NeWS. These omissions stem from the expectation that similar capabilities can be added as PostScript programs downloaded to the server. In fact, NeWS is currently distributed with a set of PostScript programs that implement most of these capabilities. These PostScript programs are not distinguished from other PostScript programs by the server, but they are special in that they perform functions that are generally considered to be system functions.

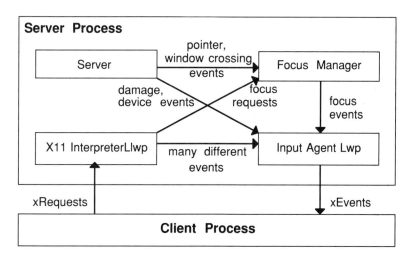

Figure: 10.3.   Event flow in X11/NeWS.

Examples of functions included in the X11 protocol but not built into NeWS are:

Keyboard Focus.

Grabs.

Selections.

Cursor confinement to a window.

Shift-modifiers, key mapping, and mouse button mapping.

One of the PostScript programs that provides system functions is called the *focus manager*. It manages the keyboard focus according to the focus model chosen by the user. There is only one incarnation of this program at any one time. The focus manager is responsible for maintaining the current input focus, and for sending *FocusIn* and *FocusOut* events when it changes.

Figure 10.4 is a high-level diagram of the flow of representative events among the server, the focus manager, the X11 interpreter, and the input agent lightweight processes. Arrows within the server process denote source and destination of events. Arrows between server and client processes denote source and destination of interprocess communication. Both of these arrows represent the same network connection; they are shown separately in order to distinguish the flow of data. The focus manager also distributes events to NeWS lightweight processes, but this is not shown.

10.6.1 Focus

In NeWS, lightweight processes that want keystrokes to go to particular canvases register those canvases with the focus manager. These canvases are called focus clients. When a focus client is notified of getting the focus, it expresses a pre-child interest in keystrokes on the root. When it is notified of losing the focus, it revokes that interest.

In X11, the focus is not the destination of keystrokes; rather it is a ceiling on bottom-up keystroke distribution. That is, if the focus window does not contain the mouse, then only the focus may get the keystrokes. However, within the focus window, keystrokes are distributed bottom-up. The focus window itself need not be interested in key presses or releases.

In X11/NeWS, when a window owned by an X11 client gets the focus, its input agent expresses an exclusive pre-child interest in keystrokes on the root, and also expresses an exclusive post-child interest on the focus window. When it loses the focus, it revokes those interests. When an event matches the first interest, the input agent looks in a dictionary maintained by the focus manager to see whether the focus contains the pointer. If the focus does not contain the pointer, the input agent specifies the focus canvas in the event; otherwise it specifies no canvas in the event. The input agent then redistributes the event, which may match X11 key press and release interests. If there are none, the interest search is terminated by the exclusive post-child interest on the focus window.

10.6.2 Active Grabs

X11 allows a client to actively grab the keyboard or the pointer. Events from the grabbed device always go to the grabbing client. A grab can specify synchronous or asynchronous mode for either or both devices. Synchronous mode for a device results in freezing that device until either a request explicitly or an event implicitly thaws it.

The input agent for a grabbing client expresses pre-child interest on the root canvas for the device it is grabbing and for the other device if the grab specified synchronous mode. When an event matches this interest, the input agent calls an X11-specific operator that buffers events for frozen devices, checks pointer events against the pointer grab event mask, translates grabbed events into X11 events, and delivers them to the grabbing client.

10.6.3 Passive Grabs

An X11 grab specified for a key or a button is a passive grab. A passive grab is specified relative to a grab-window. Pressing a mouse button activates the matching button grab on the highest grab-window between the root and the canvas under the mouse, if any exist. Pressing a key activates the matching key grab on the highest grab-window between the root and either the focus or the canvas under the mouse, depending on whether the focus contains the mouse.

A passive grab is expressed as a pre-child interest on the grab-window. Pointer events are always sent with no canvas specified in the event. Therefore, the highest pre-child interest in the ancestry of the canvas under the pointer matches, so the highest button grab gets the event. Keyboard events will always match the pre-child interest on the root corresponding to the focus. However, when the event is redistributed, the pre-child interest search is continued, so the highest key grab above either the focus or the canvas under the mouse gets the event.

When an interest for a passive grab is matched, the input agent calls an X11-specific operator, which caches the event for replay, activates the grab, and goes through active grab processing.

10.6.4 AllowEvents

The X11 *AllowEvents* request has many modes. The replay modes redistribute the cached event that activated the grab, giving lower passive grabs a chance to match. The other modes re-send buffered events, replacing them on the event queue. The event queue is ordered by timestamp. The timestamps of the buffered events are left untouched, so they are likely to be the earliest on the event queue. If the *AllowEvents* mode was synchronous, the first of these resent events to match the active grab will refreeze the device, starting the buffering all over again.

10.6.5 Crossing Events

X11 keyboard focus and window-border crossing events include more information about the relationship between the windows that the focus or cursor is exiting and entering than do analogous NeWS events. The pointer crossing code in X11/NeWS has been enhanced to put this additional information in the crossing events. In response to getting a focus event, the input agent calls an X11-specific operator, which goes through the pointer crossing code to determine the details to send the X11 client.

10.7   Selections

In general, there are two popular selection models found in various window systems: the request model, and the buffer model. In the request model, a selection service keeps track of the clients holding the various classes of selection. When a client requests information about a class of selection, the service passes that request on to the holder of the selection, or returns some means by which the requestor and the holder can communicate directly. In the buffer (clipboard) model the entire contents and attributes of a selection are transferred to the selection service, which answers requests about selections directly. The request model is more general, and handles huge selections better than the buffer model, but at the cost of client complexity and interprocess communication overhead.

X11 offers both models, provided that a convention exists whereby a client that wishes to inquire about a selection can determine which model is in use. NeWS offers a selection service implemented as a PostScript program, which provides both models transparently to an inquiring client. To preserve the ability of NeWS to support both models transparently, the selection service continues to be implemented as a PostScript program.

In X11/NeWS, the X11 interpreter implements *SetSelectionOwner*, *GetSelectionOwner*, and *ConvertSelection* requests by sending an event to the input agent, which then goes through the standard NeWS selection interface. In NeWS, set and get the selection owner are implemented by setting and getting values in a dictionary. When an X11 client becomes the selection owner, its input agent acts as the selection holder on its behalf. To implement X11 *ConvertSelection* requests, the input agent looks in the dictionary for the requested selection. If the requested selection does not exist, then the input agent delivers an X11 *SelectionNotify* event with property *None* to its client. If the selection exists, but is buffered, then the input agent delivers an X11 event with the requested contents to its client. Otherwise, the input agent sends a NeWS SelectionRequest event to the holder, which may be the input agent of an X11 client. The holding input agent converts the NeWS *SelectionRequest* event to an X11 *SelectionRequest* event and delivers the event to the holding client. It is the responsibility of the holding client to send an X11 *SelectionNotify* event to the requestor. Note that because NeWS and X11 share the selection mechanism, cut and paste between NeWS and X11 applications is possible.

Since an X11 selection is always associated with a window, but a NeWS selection does not have to be, an X11 *GetSelectionOwner* request may return null even if a selection exists. However, X11 *ConvertSelection* requests still return useful information, so this discrepancy does not seem to be worth resolving.

The X11 protocol has the concept of confining the cursor to one window, while NeWS does not. The X11/NeWS server cursor code is enhanced to implement this function for X11 only.

10.8 Modifiers

X11 clients cannot set the state of a modifier key, but NeWS clients can, which results in events being sent to X11 clients as if the hardware modifier really changed state. The set of X11 modifiers is restricted to 8, but NeWS clients may use more. The first three modifiers have a globally defined meaning for X11: *Shift*, *Lock*, and *Control*. Names for shift, lock, and control are provided so that NeWS clients may interpret these modifiers the same way as X11 clients.

Note that by expressing interest in both key presses and releases, and by inquiring the state of the keyboard on *FocusIn* and *EnterNotify*, an X11 client may keep track of the state of any keys, and therefore can interpret any number of keys as modifiers. However, only the state of the 8 modifiers is reported with each key press or release, and only the 8 modifiers can be used to qualify key grabs.

10.9   Memory Management

NeWS offers garbage collection as a form of storage management (See Section 5.8). When a lightweight process creates an object, it gets a direct reference to it. When an object ceases to be referenced, it is destroyed and its memory reclaimed. X11 uses a resource database to maintain an extra level of indirection. When an X11 client creates an object, a reference to it is stored in a resource database indexed by resource ID, and subsequently the ID is passed around. If the object is destroyed and its memory reclaimed, its resource ID will then refer to null. As long as the implementation of a request checks for null return values from resource ID look-ups, this is a robust approach.

In the X11/NeWS server, the resource database is implemented as a hierarchy of PostScript language arrays and dictionaries. To free resources after a client process has quit or "died", the dictionaries for the client's resources are removed from the resource database, normally causing them to cease to be referenced, and thereby destroyed. However, another NeWS lightweight process, most likely a system lightweight process such as the focus manager, may have obtained a valid reference to some objects in the resource database. In order to allow these other references to be flushed, the notion of a *soft reference* is introduced. An operator is provided which takes a reference to an object from the operand stack and replaces it with a soft reference to that object. When the only remaining references to an object are soft, an *Obsolete* event is sent. Any lightweight process that sets references to an object to be soft expresses interest in the *Obsolete* event for that object, and responds to a match on that interest by flushing all its references to the object.

X11 objects that may be interesting to NeWS lightweight processes are stored in the resource database as NeWS objects. For example, window and pixmap resources are represented by canvases. X11 objects that are uninteresting to NeWS lightweight processes or that do not map to NeWS object types, notably extension objects and fake objects, are stored in a new type of NeWS object, called the opaque type. An opaque object may be pushed and popped on and off the stack, saved in dictionaries and arrays, but not directly manipulated in any way.

NeWS lightweight processes are not required to associate resource IDs with the objects they create. But since the resource database consists entirely of PostScript language objects, a NeWS lightweight process has the option of creating resource IDs and associating its objects with them. By doing so, it makes its objects accessible to X11 clients. This approach is especially useful if a NeWS canvas might be managed by an X11 window manager. If a NeWS lightweight process creates an object with no resource ID, no X11 client can ever find out about it.

10.10 Connection Management

In NeWS, the loop that listens for new connections is implemented as a PostScript program, which blocks waiting for a new connection. When a connection occurs, the listening lightweight process forks a new light-weight process, which executes the file representing the connection. An X11 connection is implemented the same way, except that instead of executing the file, the listening lightweight process forks two more lightweight processes: the input agent and the X11 interpreter. The input agent is written as a PostScript program; it sits in a tight loop waiting for NeWS events, converting them to X11 events, and sending them to the X11 client. The X11 interpreter process is like a NeWS interpreter process except that instead of calling the PostScript **exec** primitive on the connection file, it calls a new primitive, **xinterp**. The **xinterp** primitive substitutes the X11 interpreter for the NeWS interpreter and then proceeds to execute the requests coming in on that connection. When the interpreter process dies, its parent lightweight process "kills" the input agent, cleans up, and dies.

10.11 Authentication

It is currently possible for the PostScript program that accepts connections to discover the name of the host the connection originated from, and to complete the connection only if that host is in a dictionary of authorized hosts. This is the level of protection offered in X11. The X11 access control requests manipulate the dictionary of authorized hosts.

10.12 Reset

The X11 protocol specifies that the server is completely reset whenever the number of its clients goes to zero, and the last client disconnects with mode set to Destroy. However, in NeWS, many lightweight processes may be active without the benefit of a connection. These processes are treated as having open connections, and some never die. For example, if the lightweight process that listens for connections died it would be impossible to connect to the server; therefore at least that process must survive.

10.13 X11/NeWS Server Differences

In most cases, X11/NeWS can operate identically as a stand-alone X11 server and as a stand-alone NeWS server, as well as allow clients of both protocols to function in perfect harmony with each other. However there are some differences between the merged server and stand-alone servers, most of which are invisible to the application.

10.13.1　X11 Differences

X11 clients do not see any difference between the X11/NeWS server and a stand-alone X11 server. Requests are interpreted exactly according to specification, events are reported exactly according to specification. However, NeWS lightweight processes that do not procure client IDs and associate resource IDs with the canvases that they create effectively hide canvases from X11 query requests. Furthermore, since some lightweight processes never die, it was considered unnecessary to reset the server after the death of all X11 clients. X11 clients cannot ever detect that the server does not reset.

10.13.2　NeWS Differences

As a side effect of the work that needed to be done to support X11, some new capabilities have been added to NeWS:

The color model for NeWS has been extended to provide modifiable color objects.

The underlying graphics system generates visibility, gravity, and unmap notification in addition to damage notification.

Pre-child interests replaced global interests.

Window crossing and focus events contain more information than they used to.

The notion of soft references has been added.

There is a minor incompatibility between previous versions of NeWS and X11/NeWS introduced by pre-child interests. In NeWS1.1, if a canvas was specified in a sent event, then the global interest list was not searched when distributing that event. In X11/NeWS, the pre-child interests of the ancestors of the canvas specified in a sent event are always searched. Window crossing and focus events are also not backwards compatible. Other than this, the changes are upwardly compatible.

10.14 Summary

The X11/NeWS server design takes advantage of the great degree of commonality between the requirements of the X11 protocol and the requirements of the NeWS protocol. In X11/NeWS, one scheduler allocates time between clients of both protocols. One homogeneous window forest allocates screen resources between windows created by both protocols. One homogeneous event queue provides orderly distribution of events between clients of both protocols. One window manager is provided that presents an integrated user interface for manipulating all windows created by clients of both protocols. One keyboard focus manager is provided that presents an integrated user interface for directing keystrokes among clients of both protocols. One selection service provides exchange of data between clients of both protocols. Programs written to use either X11 protocol or NeWS protocol run unmodified, coexisting in an environment that presents an integrated interface to the user.

I
Description of the Plates

All 8 plates are screen dumps from NeWS or X11/NeWS running on various color workstations.

Plate 1. NeWS running on the Parallax Graphics Viper display, as described in section 9.2, can display live video in NeWS windows. The windows showing the space shuttle and the Viper board itself are live video windows; note how they overlap and are overlapped by normal NeWS windows, such as the pop-up menu controlling the video.

Plate 2. A Silicon Graphics IRIS running the NeWS-based 4sight window system. The server supports normal NeWS clients, such as the calculator, and also clients using SGI's GL library to access the display hardware directly, such as those drawing in the triangular and oval windows. The server uses the IRIS clip hardware to restrict these high-performance 3D programs to drawing within the NeWS windows using the techniques described in section 9.3.2. Note the window borders, showing SGI's "house style" implemented as a sub-class of *LiteWindow*.

Plate 3. This and the next plate show the NeWS-based human interface of a well log interpretation workstation. They are reproduced by permission of Schlumberger Technology Corporation. All the windows are described declaratively in a Lisp-based system that generates code to send to the NeWS server at run-time, using Schlumberger's multiple-inheritance extensions to the class mechanism of Chapter 6.

The green window (top-left corner) shows a "map" of the oil wells from which data is available. The user clicked on the icon to select a well, and the beige window showed its characteristics and the trips (one in this case) made to gather data from it. The upper white window shows general information about the trip, and the blue window shows the five times instruments were lowered into the hole. The lower white window shows details of one of the instruments.

Plate 4. These windows show the data gathered by various instruments as they were lowered into the hole. The right-most region shows the entire depth interval for which data was collected, with the scroll bar showing in orange the area displayed in detail in the rest of the window. Various scrolling modes, including continuous, page, and thumb, are implemented entirely in NeWS. The user selected a curve (the left-most blue one) which caused a graphic attributes editor to appear (yellow window). Clicking on an item (the color of the curve) pops up an appropriate menu (the color menu) to modify the selected graphic attribute.

Plate 5.   This and the next plate show the NeWS Cookbook, a hypertext containing NeWS reference material and examples implemented in NeWS by Pica Pty. Ltd of Woolloomooloo in Australia. The spiral-bound notebook (note the spiral-shaped window) can be read sequentially, or the index tabs at the side allow quick selection of topics, or the user can click on any text in italic to follow a link to another page. Pages can be ''torn off'' and left visible for easy reference.

The window at the top left is the cookbook itself, open to the contents page, but the other two pages have been torn off (note the top edge). The user clicked on the words *Fob Watch* to start the ''Tempus Fugit'' clock client, part of whose *cps* code is visible in the lower right page (see Chapter 7).

Plate 6.   The cookbook is open to a page describing a factory simulation example. Below is a control panel for the simulation, implemented with the *LiteItem* sliders and switches described in Chapter 6. The lower left window shows the progress of the simulation, with dynamically updated images of the valves and tanks, and graphs.

Plate 7.   AT&T's OPEN LOOK graphical user interface specification has been implemented in a number of ways. These three NeWS applications use OPEN LOOK sub-classes of *Lite*. The two lower windows are the main window of a paint program implemented entirely in NeWS, and the property sheet that sets the size and color of its brush. Lon Chaney appears courtesy of a NeWS-based hypertext browser - the contents of each card can be either text or PostScript programs. The spline curves outlining parts of the face in the top right window are generated by an experimental drawing program; they allow the user to trace parts of an image by adjusting the control points of the splines, and output PostScript programs generating the shapes.

Plate 8.   The X11/NeWS server, described in Chapter 10, runs both X and NeWS applications. The user is unaware of the protocol used by an application; the window systems coexist completely.

The characters on the screen, drawn by both NeWS and X, were scan-converted on-the-fly from outlines. Open Fonts Type-maker makes it easy for font suppliers to generate "intelligent" outlines in the F3 format, like the New Century Schoolbook and Snell Roundhand examples here, which can be read by TypeScaler in the X11/NeWS server. The window with the grid shows an expanded view of an outline A, and the result of TypeScaler scan-converting it 20 pixels high. The window at the right shows New Century Schoolbook Roman in a range of sizes. These, and the "Text Sample" windows, were drawn by NeWS applications.

To the lower left is Fileview, a X11 directory browser imple-mented using Sun's XView X11 toolkit. This too uses outline fonts generated by TypeScaler.

The window borders for both X and NeWS applications are provided by an OPEN LOOK window manager written entirely in NeWS. It provides NeWS clients with a class, similar to LiteWindow, from which they can subclass their top-level win-dows. And it behaves like a normal X11 window manager, intercepting a client's attempt to map its top-level window and reparenting it to be a child of a decoration canvas.

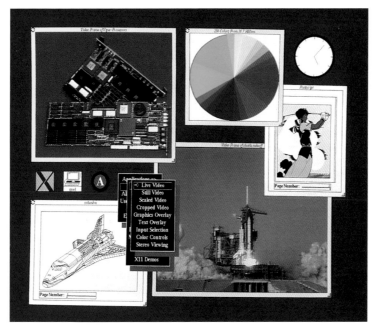

Plate 1.   Live video of the space shuttle launch and of the Parallax
            Graphics Inc. Viper board on which pNeWS is running.

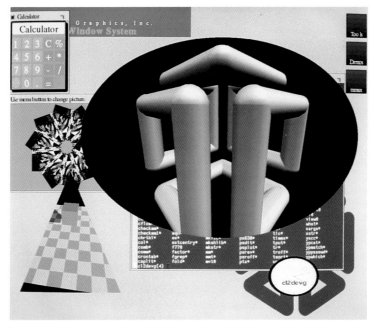

Plate 2.   Silicon Graphics IRIS running 4sight, with high-performance
            3D graphics in triangular and oval NeWS windows.

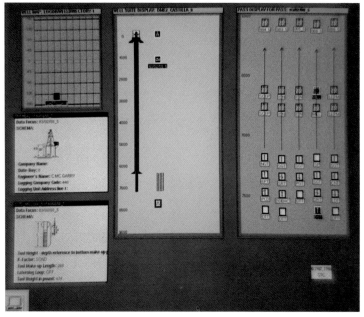

Plate 3.   Top-level human interface of Schlumberger well log interpretation workstation.

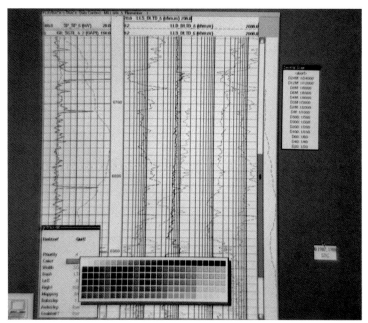

Plate 4.   A lower level of the Schlumberger interface, showing data from instruments lowered into the well.

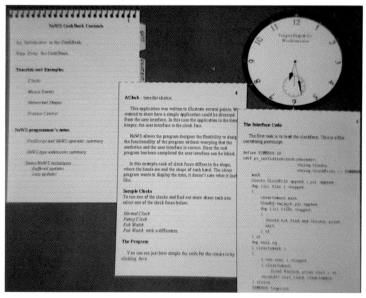

Plate 5.   The NeWS Cookbook, open to the contents page, and two
torn-off pages describing the *Fob Watch* example.

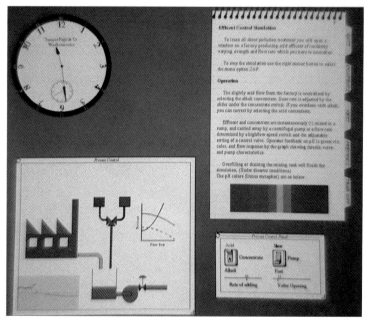

Plate 6.   Another page from the NeWS Cookbook, describing the
factory simulation running in the lower two windows.

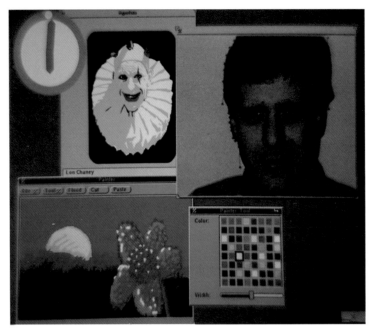

Plate 7.　　　OPEN LOOK applications implemented in NeWS.

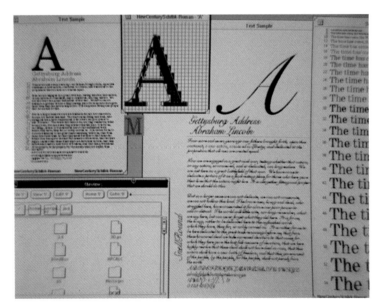

Plate 8.　　　OPEN LOOK applications implemented in both X and NeWS, on X11/NeWS, all using Open Fonts outline font technology.

Bibliography

[ADOB85a] Adobe Systems, Inc., *PostScript Language Reference Manual.* Adobe Systems, Inc., Addison-Wesley, 1985.

[ADOB85b] Adobe Systems, Inc., *PostScript Language Tutorial and Cookbook.* Adobe Systems, Inc., Addison-Wesley, 1985.

[AKEL88] Akeley, K., Jermoluk, T., *High-Performance Polygon Rendering*, Proceedings of SIGGRAPH '88, Atlanta GA, August 1988, published as *Computer Graphics* **22**(4), pp. 239-246.

[CARD85] Cardelli, L., Pike R., *Squeak — A Language for Communicating with Mice*, Proceedings of SIGGRAPH '85, San Francisco CA, July 1985, published as *Computer Graphics* **19**(3), pp. 199-204.

[DENS86] Densmore, O. M., *Object Oriented Programming in NeWS*, Proceedings of the Third Usenix Computer Graphics Workshop, Monterey CA, November 1986.

[ESPI87] Espinosa, A.C., and Rose, A.C., *QuickDraw: A Programmer's Guide*, Apple Computer, March 1987.

[FISH87] Fisher, B., *X11 Server Extensions Engineering Specification.* Digital Equipment Corporation, August 1987.

[GETT86] Gettys, J., *Problems Implementing Window Systems in UNIX*, Proceedings of Winter 1986 Usenix, Denver CO, January 1986, pp. 89-97.

[GOLD83] Goldberg, A., Robsin, D., *Smalltalk-80: The Language and its Implementation*, Addison-Wesley, May 1983.

[GOSL86] Gosling, J., *SUNDEW: A Distributed and Extensible Window System*, Proceedings of Winter 1986 Usenix, Denver CO, January 1986, pp. 89-97.

[HOAR78] Hoare, C.A.R., *Communicating Sequential Processes*, Communications of the ACM **21**(8), August 1978, pp. 666-677.

[HOPK88] Hopkins, D., Callahan, J., Weiser, M, Shneiderman, B., *A Comparative Analysis of Pie Menu Performance*, Proceedings ACM CHI '88 Conference, Washington D.C. 1988.

224

[HOPK89]   Hopkins, D., Callahan, J., Weiser, M., *Pies: Implementation, Evaluation, and Application of Circular Menus*, To appear in Communications of the ACM, 1989.

[LAMP88]   Lampson, B., *Personal Distributed Computing: Alto and Ethernet Software*, in Goldberg, A. (ed) *A History of Personal Workstations*, ACM Press History Series, 1988.

[LEFF88]   Leffler, S., *A Window on the Future*, UNIX Review, **6**(6), June 1988, pp. 62-69.

[LIPK82]   Lipkie, D. E., et al., *Star Graphics: An Object-Oriented Implementation*, Proceedings of SIGGRAPH '82, Boston MA, July 1982, published as *Computer Graphics* **16**(3), pp. 115-124.

[MORR86]   Morris, J. et. al., *Andrew: A Distributed Personal Computing Environment*, Communications of the ACM **29**(3), March 1986.

[PHIL87]   Phillips, R.L., Forslund, D.W., *Using the NeWS Window System in a Cray Environment*, Los Alamos National Laboratory, Los Alamos, NM, May 1987. Presented at Cray User's Group, New York NY.

[PRAT85]   Pratt, V., *Techniques for Conic Splines*, Proceedings of SIGGRAPH '85, San Francisco CA, July 1985, published as *Computer Graphics* **19**(3), pp. 151-159.

[ROBE87]   Roberts W. T., et al., *First Impressions of NeWS*, Eurographics Forum, 1988.

[ROBE88]   Roberts, W. T., et al., *NeWS and X, Beauty and the Beast?*, Dept. of Computer Science, Queen Mary College, London, July 1988.

[ROSE87]   Rosenthal, D.S.H., Gosling, J., *A Window Manager for Bitmapped Displays and Unix*, in Methodology of Window Management Systems, edited by Hopgood, F.R.A. et al., Springer-Verlag, 1986.

[ROSE89]   Rosenthal D. S. H., *X Window System, Version 11: Inter-Client Communication Conventions Manual*, MIT X Consortium, Cambridge MA, 1989.

[SCHA88]   Schaufler R., *X11/NeWS Design Overview*, Proceedings of Summer 1988 Usenix Conference, July 1988, pp. 23-35.

[SCHE86]   Scheifler, R. W., Gettys, J., *The X Window System*. ACM Transactions on Graphics, **5**(2), April 1986, pp. 79-109.

[SCHE87]   Scheifler, R. W., *X Window System Protocol Specification, Version 11.* Massachusetts Institute of Technology, Cambridge, MA and Digital Equipment Corporation, Maynard, MA, 1987.

[SCHE88]   Scheifler R. W., Gettys J., Newman, R., *X Window System: C Library and Protocol Reference*, Digital Press, 1988.

[SUN87a]   Sun Microsystems, Inc., *NeWS 1.1 Manual.* Sun Microsystems, Inc., PN 800-2146-10, 1987.

[SUN87b]   Sun Microsystems, Inc., *NeWS Technical Overview.* Sun Microsystems, Inc., PN 800-1498-05, 1987.

[SUN85]   Sun Microsystems, Inc., *Programmer's Reference Manual for SunWindows*, Sun Microsystems, Inc., April, 1985.

[THAC88]   Thacker, C., *Personal Distributed Computing: The Alto and Ethernet Hardware*, in Goldberg, A. (ed) *A History of Personal Workstations*, ACM Press History Series, 1988.

[WARN82]   Warnock, J., Wyatt, D., *A Device Independent Graphics Imaging Model for Use with Raster Devices,* Proceedings of SIGGRAPH '82, Boston MA, July 1982, published as *Computer Graphics* **16**(3), pp. 313-319.

Index

F

F3 221
Farrell, Jerry vi
Fileview 221
fill 70, 74, 76
findfont 75
flatness 77
flexibility 4
floor 58
Flynn, Anthony vi
focus
    click-to-type 48
    focus-follows-cursor 48
    in X11/NeWS 210
focus-follows-cursor 48
font 77, 169
    in X11/NeWS 205
    outline 74, 206, 221
    problems of X10 model 18
for 66
forall 66
fork 93, 95
Freedman, Francesca vi

G

garbage collection 111
    in X11/NeWS 214
ge 59
GEM 37
Geometry Engine 187
Geschke, Charles v, 8, 12
get 60, 64
getcanvaslocation 85
Gettys, Jim 37
Gilmore, John vi
Gosling, James 11, 34, 38
grab 210
    active in X11/NeWS 211
    passive in X11/NeWS 211
graphic state stack 56
graphics 5
graphics library 49
graphics operations 68

graphics state 76
gravity, window 203
grestore 76, 82
gsave 76, 82
gt 59

H

halftone screen 77
Hall, Mark vi
heavyweight process 32, 93
Hickmann, Kipp vi
hierarchy 84
Hoeber, Tony v
Hopkins, Don vi, 146
HSB 111
hsbcolor 111
hypertext 220

I

IBM 34, 37
    PC 178, 193
    PC/RT 34, 35
    VM 51
idiv 58
if 66
ifelse 66
image 73, 92
imagecanvas 92
imagemask 73
imaging 72
imaging model 49, 68
    Cedar Graphics 30
    in X11/NeWS 204
index 59
Information Technology Center 34
inheritance 120
initclip 88
input agent 207, 211
input devices 47
input focus 48, 210
insertcanvasabove 85
insertcanvasbelow 85
interest 98, 99, 145, 207, 210,

234